The SYBEX

VENTURA
INSTANT
REFERENCE

The SYBEX Prompter Series

We've designed the SYBEX Prompter Series to meet the evolving needs of software users, who want essential information presented in an accessible format. Our best authors have distilled their expertise into compact *Instant Reference* books you can use to look up the precise use of any command—its syntax, available options, and operation. More than just summaries, these books also provide realistic examples and insights into effective usage drawn from our authors' wealth of experience.

The SYBEX Prompter Series also includes these titles:

Lotus 1-2-3 Instant Reference
Greg Harvey and Kay Yarborough Nelson

WordPerfect Instant Reference
Greg Harvey and Kay Yarborough Nelson

WordPerfect 5 Instant Reference
Greg Harvey and Kay Yarborough Nelson

dBASE Instant Reference
Alan Simpson

Turbo BASIC Instant Reference
Douglas Hergert

DOS Instant Reference
Greg Harvey and Kay Yarborough Nelson

HyperTalk Instant Reference
Greg Harvey

WordStar Instant Reference
David J. Clark

The SYBEX Prompter™ Series

VENTURA™ INSTANT REFERENCE

Matthew Holtz

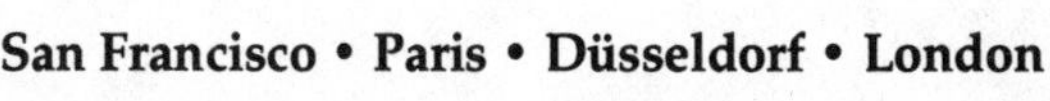

The SYBEX Prompter Series
Editor in Chief: Rudolph S. Langer
Managing Editor: Barbara Gordon
Series Editor: James A. Compton
Editor: Alan Hislop

Cover design by Thomas Ingalls + Associates
Series design by Ingrid Owen
Technical illustrations by Lucie Zivny and Jeffrey Giese

Library of Congress Card Number: **88-62828**
ISBN **0-89588-544-1**
Manufactured in the United States of America
10 9 8 7 6 5 4 3 2 1

ACKNOWLEDGMENTS

Thanks to the SYBEX staff members and freelancers who assisted in the production of the book. Alan Hislop was the copy editor and Jim Compton the series editor. Mark Taber was the technical reviewer. Jocelyn Reynolds and Bob Myren did the word processing, and Charles Cowens the page composition. Jeff Giese and Lucie Zivny did the artwork, and Sonja Schenk handled the screen reproduction. Sylvia Townsend headed the proofreading crew. Hannah Robinson also provided valuable suggestions.

Special thanks also to Brenda Beck, at Hill and Knowlton, for providing software used in writing this book.

Table of Contents

Appendices

INTRODUCTION

Xerox Ventura Publisher has become the most popular desktop publishing program for IBM and compatible personal computers. It is the standard against which people measure other desktop publishers. One reason for Ventura's popularity is the thoroughness of its capabilities. At the same time, many users find that they need these capabilities under severe deadlines, a hallmark of publishing. Thus, because of Ventura's complexity and the requirements that publishing imposes, the need for a handy guide, useful in any case, is all the more pressing.

In this book, our goal is to provide quick answers to questions that arise in your day-to-day work with Ventura. When you need instant solutions, turn to this book and find the topic you need.

The entries are presented alphabetically, with subject headings that reflect the applications that you may require, or the tasks you need to accomplish, rather than the way the program is constructed. Complete cross-referencing allows you to follow any topic through all of its aspects. For a more complete understanding of how the book is organized, you may find it beneficial to browse through the Table of Contents.

For each operation or feature you will find the following information:

- the Ventura release in which the feature is available
- a sequence of steps showing at a glance the exact keystrokes, menu selections, or mouse operations to use in carrying out the procedure in each of its variant forms
- a usage discussion explaining how the step sequence works, noting any rules or restrictions that apply to the feature and offering valuable tips on using it effectively
- brief instructions for undoing the operation
- a list of any related entries you can consult for further information

Broader topics are divided into sections on individual operations as needed; these sections also contain the items listed above. Most entries also present simple examples, but some features cannot be adequately illustrated within the confines of a compact reference.

To help you quickly find the information you need, main entry names appear in the page headers; section titles within these entries (such as "Adjusting Footnote Frames" within **Footnotes**) are listed in the Table of Contents.

You can also find a variety of helpful reference matter in the appendices and inside covers.

This book is geared to the person who has had some exposure to Ventura. It assumes that the program is installed; however, since you may need to reinstall Ventura if you add hardware to your system, Appendix A briefly outlines that procedure. It also assumes knowledge of how to use the dialog boxes and Item Selector boxes, although these and other screen elements are detailed in Appendix B. While an understanding of Ventura's fundamental operations is helpful, for readers who need a refresher, such basic tasks as switching the operating mode are presented in the appropriate sections.

This book covers versions 2.0, 1.1, and 1.0 of Xerox Ventura Publisher. There is some emphasis on version 2.0, but all procedures list the steps for each version. Some of the material is shared with a companion book for readers who need a more step-by-step approach to learning the program, *Mastering Ventura,* also published by SYBEX.

Good luck with your desktop publishing. And keep this book handy whenever you use Ventura.

Alignment

You can specify the horizontal alignment of paragraphs as left-aligned, right-aligned, justified, centered, or decimal; you can specify vertical alignment as top, middle, or bottom.

Horizontal Alignment

VERSION

2.0, 1.1, 1.0 (Decimal setting 2.0 only)

SEQUENCE OF STEPS

Paragraph mode
[select a paragraph]
Paragraph menu
Alignment
Horz Alignment: **Left, Center, Right, Justified** or **Decimal**
OK or ↵
[tag other paragraphs as desired]

USAGE

The horizontal alignment of a paragraph determines whether its text is flush, ragged, centered, or decimal-aligned. Text that is flush along both the left and right edges is said to be *justified*. Left-aligned text is flush on the left edge and ragged on the right edge. Right-aligned text is flush on the right and ragged on the left. Decimal-aligned text lines up the text according to the (first) decimal point in each line of text.

To set or adjust the alignment of a paragraph (and of all identically tagged paragraphs) in the Paragraph mode, select a paragraph whose alignment you wish to adjust by clicking it with the mouse. All paragraphs with the same tag will be modified as well (see **Tags**). Select the Paragraph menu and choose **Alignment**. In the dialog box that appears, set Horz Alignment to **Left**, **Center**, **Right**, **Justified**, or **Decimal**, according to the alignment you desire. Then click **OK** or press ↵ to register your choice.

If you choose **Decimal** alignment, you can provide a value for In From Right To Decimal. This value will determine the distance that the decimal point is positioned from the right edge of the paragraph, as set by the Paragraph menu's Spacing dialog box with the In From Right setting. Normally, Ventura uses a period for the decimal point; you can change that with Options menu/Set Preferences (see **Options**).

TIP

Use decimal alignment, available with version 2.0, as a quick way to line up decimals without using tabs. To use decimal tabs, see **Tables**.

UNDO

With the paragraph selected, select the Paragraph menu and choose **Alignment**. Change the Horz Alignment setting back (the "plainest" setting is Left) and give the OK.

SEE ALSO

Indents; Tables; Tags

Vertical Alignment

VERSION

2.0 only

SEQUENCE OF STEPS

Paragraph mode
[select a paragraph]
Alignment
Vert Alignment: **Top** or **Middle** or **Bottom**
OK or ↵
[tag other paragraphs as desired]

USAGE

The vertical alignment of a paragraph determines whether Ventura places the paragraph at the top, middle, or bottom of its containing area, such as the frame it occupies (including the underlying-page frame). Ventura positions the paragraph within the space left over by the top and bottom margins (assigned with the Frame menu, Margins & Columns dialog box). Vertical alignment also determines the placement of Box Text within its corresponding box. Vertical alignment is assigned by the tag: all similarly tagged paragraphs receive the same treatment.

TIP

When you set Vert Alignment to **Middle**, a paragraph so tagged will appear in the middle of the space that remains, following any Top-aligned paragraphs above it. Any paragraph that follows a Middle paragraph or a Bottom paragraph appears on the next page or in a succeeding frame that's assigned the same text file. It will not normally appear on the same page or in the same frame or Box Text box as the Middle or Bottom paragraph before it. However, when a frame appears within a frame (including within the underlying page frame), Ventura will use the top and bottom edges of the inside frame to set off alignment areas for the outside frame.

UNDO

With the paragraph selected, select the Paragraph menu and choose **Alignment**. Change the Vert Alignment setting (Top is the most standard) and give the OK.

SEE ALSO

Margins; Tags

Anchoring Frames

Anchor a frame to tie it to a position in the text.

VERSION

2.0, 1.1

USAGE

Usually you use an anchored frame to keep a picture, within its frame, with the text that references it. First, you provide an anchor name to the frame for a reference. Then you insert that name in the text as an anchor. Before printing, you use the re-anchor procedure described below to reunite frames with their anchors in the text.

Assigning Anchor Names

SEQUENCE OF STEPS

Frame mode or also (2.0 only) **Graphics** Mode
[select a frame]
Frame menu
Anchors & Captions
[provide an anchor name]
OK or ↵

USAGE

To provide an anchor name for a frame that you want to anchor, first use the **Frame** mode to select the frame. Then use the **Frame** menu and choose **Anchors & Captions**. In the Anchor field, provide a name. Then click **OK** or press ↵. Use the same steps to change the anchor name.

TIP

Although you can click the Inserts buttons in this dialog box to use the codes for figure number, table number, and so on as part of the anchor name, it's usually better not to. Ventura will use the code literally and position the frame with a matching anchor, which could be quite confusing. It's best to use a short name (maximum is 16 characters) descriptive of the frame's contents, such as "income graph."

UNDO

With the frame selected, use the Frame menu and choose **Anchors & Captions**. To remove the name from the Anchor field, press the Esc key.

SEE ALSO

Frames; Pictures

Inserting and Editing Anchors in Text

SEQUENCE OF STEPS

To insert a frame's anchor into text:

Text mode
[click location in text]

(Version 2.0)	(Version 1.1)
Ctrl-C or	**Edit** menu
Edit menu / **Ins Special Item**	
F5 or **Frame Anchor**	**Insert/Edit Anchor**

[enter anchor name]
[click a button for Frame's New Location]
OK or ↵

To edit an existing anchor in the text:

Text mode
[position the text cursor directly before the anchor]

(Version 2.0)
Ctrl-D or
Edit menu / **Edit Special Item**

(Version 1.1)
Edit menu
Insert/Edit Anchor

[adjust settings]
OK or ↵

USAGE

To insert an anchor into text, in the **Text** mode click the spot in text that you want to associate with the frame. Then, in version 2.0, either use the Edit menu and choose **Insert Special Item** or simply press **Ctrl-C**. From the resulting menu, choose **Frame Anchor** or press **F5**. The Insert / Edit Anchor dialog box appears. In version 1.1, you can simply select **Insert/Edit Anchor** from the Edit menu.

In the dialog box, enter the anchor name you provided for the frame you want to associate with the text, and then click one of the buttons for Frame's New Location. To keep the frame on the same page as the anchor in text, but always in the same position on the page, choose **Fixed, On Same Page As Anchor**. To position the frame on the same page but always directly below the line of text containing the anchor, select **Relative, Below Anchor Line**. You can also position the frame above the line of text by choosing **Relative, Above Anchor Line**. With version 2.0 you can use **Relative, Automatically At Anchor** to insert small icons, pictures, symbols, or graphics (tied to the frame) directly within the line of text that contains the anchor name.

When you click **OK** or press ↵, Ventura will insert the anchor into the text. If Tabs and Returns are showing (see **Options**) you'll see a small degree symbol (°) indicating the anchor. When the anchor is to the right of the text cursor, the words *Frame Anchor* appear in the Current box toward the bottom of the Side-bar.

You can make changes in the dialog box for an existing frame anchor and edit the frame anchor's name and location. Place the text cursor directly in front of the frame anchor. The words *Frame Anchor* should appear in the Current box. Then, with version 2, press Ctrl-D or use the Edit menu to select **Edit Special Item**. In version 1.1, use the Edit menu and select **Insert/Edit Anchor**.

UNDO

To remove an anchor from text, select the anchor by positioning the text cursor to the left of the anchor. The words *Frame Anchor* should appear in the Current box. Press the Del key to remove the anchor. If desired, you can then paste the anchor elsewhere in text, along with the settings in the Insert/Edit Anchor dialog box (see **Cut/Copy/Paste**).

SEE ALSO

Cut/Copy/Paste; Text

Reanchoring Frames

SEQUENCE OF STEPS

Chapter menu (2.0) or **Page** menu (1.1)
Re-Anchor Frames
This Page or **All Pages**

USAGE

This procedure properly repositions frames with their associated anchors in text. Use the Chapter menu and choose **Reanchor Frames**. In the dialog box that appears, click **All Pages** to scan the entire document and reposition all the frames. Click **This Page** to reposition the frames on the current page only. If you need to reposition only the frames on the current page, using **This Page** will often save time.

When reanchoring the frames in a chapter, Ventura may place the frames in undesirable locations—in margins or on top of one another, for example. Before printing, be sure to check the entire document for proper positioning of the frames.

UNDO

Because Ventura provides no direct way to return the document to its condition before reanchoring, you should save your document immediately before you reanchor. Then, if the results you obtain are undesirable, you can use File menu /Abandon to retrieve the saved version.

Inserting Anchors with your Word Processor

SEQUENCE OF STEPS

Frame Fixed, On Same Page As Anchor:

<$&_anchor name_ **>**

Frame Relative, Below Anchor Line:

<$&_anchor name_ **[v]>**

Frame Relative, Above Anchor Line:

<$&_anchor name_ **[^]>**

Frame Relative, Automatically At Anchor:

<$&_anchor name_ **[-]>**

USAGE

Use the text codes given above to insert anchors into text with your word processor. For *anchor name,* substitute the anchor name assigned to the frame that you want Ventura to use at that location. For example, to place an anchor that will cause the frame to appear in a relative position above the line that holds the anchor, you enter a left angle bracket (<), followed by a dollar sign ($), an ampersand (&), the name you've assigned to the frame's anchor, then a left bracket ([), a (Shift-6) caret (^), a right bracket (]), and a right angle bracket (>).

UNDO

Use your word processor to delete the inserted code sequence. You can also use Ventura to remove the anchor from text as described above.

EXAMPLE

<$&income graph[^]>The coded sequence at the beginning of this sentence causes the frame with the income graph to appear above this sentence.

SEE ALSO

Text; Frames

Arrows

To draw arrows, see **Line Drawing.**
To use the keypad arrows, see **Text.**

Attributes

Frame attributes, see **Frames**.
Paragraph tag attributes, see **Tags**.
Graphics attributes, see **Graphics**.
Text attributes, see **Text**.

Backgrounds

Frame backgrounds, see **Frames**.
Graphics backgrounds (fill attributes), see **Graphics**.

Big First Character

You can start selected paragraphs with an oversize first character, either dropped or raised.

VERSION

2.0,1.1,1.0

SEQUENCE OF STEPS

Paragraph mode
[select a paragraph]
Paragraph menu
Special Effects
Special Effect: **Big First Char**
Commands: **Set Font Properties**
[increase size]
OK or ↵
[tag other paragraphs if desired]

USAGE

In Ventura's terminology, a big first character is a character, at the beginning of a paragraph, that is set in a font larger than the font used for the rest of the paragraph. This paragraph has a big first character. Often, this effect is used for the first paragraph of a chapter or magazine article. You set this feature by the tag.

When a big first character displaces the beginning lines of text in a paragraph, it is called a *dropped capital*. When it extends above the paragraph, it is called a *stickup initial*.

To add a big first character to one or more paragraphs, first activate the Paragraph mode. Then select a sample paragraph (one that you want to provide with a big first character) by clicking it with the mouse. All paragraphs so tagged will be modified as well (see **Tags**). Pull down the Paragraph menu and choose **Special Effects**. Select **Big First Char** and then Commands: **Set Font Properties**. Increase the value for Size; sizes available depend on the width table you're using (see **Fonts**). Adjust other characteristics for the big first character, if you want to. For example, you may want to provide a value to shift up (raise) the character. You can also adjust the Face, Style (italic, bold), color or Shift Down (to lower the character). Then click **OK** or press ↵.

Normally the big first character displaces text to create a dropped capital. However, starting with version 1.1, you can use the Special Effects dialog box to decrease the number of lines that the Big First Character occupies and thereby create a stickup initial. In the Space for Big First setting, click **Custom** (rather than **Normal**) and then provide a value smaller than the amount Ventura normally allots (only 1 line, for example). When set, give the OK.

You will usually want only the first paragraph of a chapter or section to have a big first character, with other paragraph attributes the same as for the remaining paragraphs. Therefore, set the tag for the other text first (usually Body Text), and then add a new tag for the big first character effect, copying attributes from the Body Text tag (see **Tags**).

UNDO

With the paragraph selected, use the Paragraph menu and choose **Special Effects**. Select Special Effect: **None** and give the OK.

SEE ALSO

Fonts; Tags

Boldface

You can print characters or blocks of text in **boldface** type.

VERSION

2.0, 1.1, 1.0

USAGE

You can set boldface in several ways, depending on the type and extent of the material you want boldfaced. You can boldface entire paragraphs by the tag, which affects all paragraphs so tagged, or you can assign boldface to one or more characters within a paragraph, either with Ventura menu options or when entering text with your word processor. You can also assign boldface to special features, like big first characters; use the Set Font Properties command associated with the feature you want.

Boldfacing with Paragraph Tags

SEQUENCE OF STEPS

Paragraph mode
[select a paragraph]
Paragraph menu
Font
Style: **Bold**
OK or ↵
[tag other paragraphs if desired]

USAGE

Using tags will make all characters in the selected paragraph—and all similarly tagged paragraphs—change to boldface. In Paragraph mode, select a sample paragraph that you want to boldface. Use the Paragraph menu and choose **Font**. In the dialog box that appears, under the Style heading, choose **Bold**. Note that Bold may not be available (as indicated by ghosting) in all faces and sizes.

UNDO

With the paragraph tagged, use the Paragraph menu and choose **Font**. Change Style to **Normal** or some setting other than Bold and give the OK.

SEE ALSO

Fonts; Tags

Boldfacing Selected Text

SEQUENCE OF STEPS

Text mode
[select the text]
Assignment List: **Bold**

or

Text mode
[select the text]
Set Font button
Style: **Bold**
OK or ↵

USAGE

You can boldface selected text by using the **Bold** setting on the Side-bar or by using a font dialog box. In either case, first activate the Text mode (see **Text**), and then use the mouse to select the text for boldfacing. To use the first method, you then simply click **Bold** on the Assignment list that appears on the Side-bar when Ventura is in the Text mode. To use the second method, you then click the **Set Font** button, which also appears on the Side-bar in Text mode. In the dialog box that appears, under the Style heading click **Bold**. Then give the OK. Boldface may not be available in all faces and sizes.

UNDO

See the instructions under "Assigning Fonts to Selected Text" in **Fonts.**

SEE ALSO

Fonts

Boldfacing with the Word Processor

SEQUENCE OF STEPS

<B>*[text]***<D>**

or

[use supported word processor's boldface procedure]

USAGE

If Ventura supports boldface from your word processor, you can use the word processor's method for boldfacing text. The text will appear in boldface in Ventura and still appear in boldface when you look at the text file with the word processor. See **Text** for more information on using Ventura with word processors.

If Ventura does not support boldface from your word processor, place the code **<B>** at the beginning of the text to appear in boldface. Placing the code **<D>** at the end of the boldface will cause the text to return to normal (as set by the paragraph tag) at that point.

You can eliminate this ending code if the effect continues to the end of the paragraph, because the boldfacing will end when the paragraph ends unless there is another <B> code at the beginning of the next paragraph. You can also eliminate the ending code if boldface ends when another effect begins; a new code supersedes any previous codes (see **Fonts**).

UNDO

Use your word processor's delete capabilities to remove the codes. You can also remove the effect in Ventura by following the Undo procedures given above.

EXAMPLE

This is normal. <B>This is bold.<D> This is normal again.

would be printed by Ventura as

This is normal. **This is bold.** This is normal again.

SEE ALSO

Text

Boxes

You can create boxes associated with a paragraph tag, those that are part of a frame, free-form boxes created with the Graphics mode, and, with version 2.0, box characters.

VERSION

2.0, 1.1, 1.0 (Box characters, 2.0 only)

Boxes as Part of a Frame

SEQUENCE OF STEPS

Frame mode or also (2.0 only) **Graphics** mode
[select a frame]
Frame menu
Ruling Box Around
[set width, height, other features]
OK or ↵

USAGE

With Ventura in the **Frame** mode, select a frame that you want to box. Use the **Frame** menu and choose **Ruling Box Around**. You'll see the dialog box in Figure 1. For Width, select **Frame** (the only width, besides None, available for frames). Set the Color and Pattern as desired. White will not show unless it's

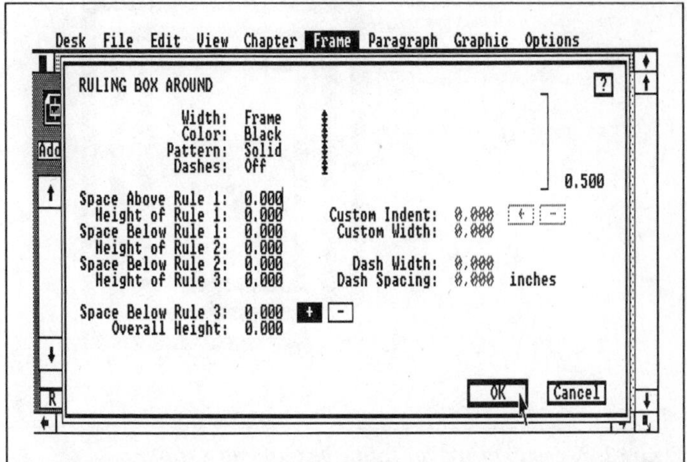

Figure 1: Ruling Box Around dialog box

against a dark background (which you can set with the Frame menu's Frame Background dialog box). For more information on color, see **Color**; for more information on patterns, see **Graphics**.

Starting with Rule 1, set the Height (thickness) of up to 3 rules (see Figure 2). Set the space between the rules. The Space Below Rule 3 setting does not apply to frames here.

As you provide these settings, samples of the boxes will appear in the dialog box. However, the sample (including the spacing) is twice the size that it appears in the document. Only the first half-inch of boxes appear in the sample. Thus, if your settings are more than one-half inch, the sample may not appear (though the document will be affected nonetheless).

The Overall Height indicator displays the total of the values set above it. Thus, it indicates the total thickness of the lines and spacing that compose one edge of the box.

To be sure that text or other material that appears within a frame does not conflict with the box, you must provide the frame with margins great enough to accommodate the box.

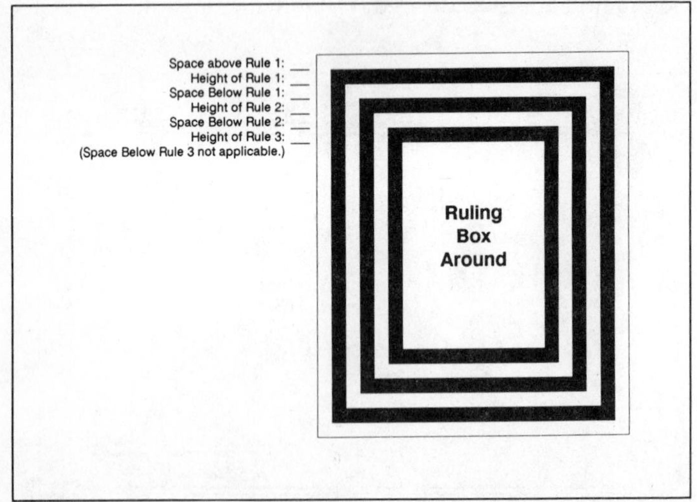

Figure 2: Measurements for ruling box around a frame

Use the Frame menu's Margins & Columns dialog box to adjust the margins of the frame to keep them free of text.

To create a box made up of dashes, set Dashes: **On**. Then provide values for Dash Width (length of a dash) and Dash Spacing (the distance between dashes). Other settings (Custom Indent, Custom Width) don't apply in Frame mode.

UNDO

With the frame selected, use the Frame menu and choose **Ruling Box Around**. Set Width to **None** and give the OK.

SEE ALSO

Frames; Margins

Boxes Associated with Paragraph Tags

SEQUENCE OF STEPS

Paragraph mode
[select a paragraph]
Paragraph menu
Ruling Box Around
[set width, height, other features]
OK or ↵
[tag other paragraphs if desired]

USAGE

When you assign boxes by the paragraph tag, all paragraphs so tagged will be boxed in the same manner.

In Paragraph mode, select a sample paragraph that you want to box. Use the Paragraph menu and choose **Ruling Box Around**. In the resulting dialog box, set the features as discussed under "Boxes as Part of a Frame."

There are other Width alternatives, ghosting in Frame mode, that become available in Paragraph mode. Under Width, choose **Text** if you want the box to be the same width as the text of the paragraphs. Choose **Margin** and Ventura sets the box according to the paragraph's In From Left and In From Right values (that you've assigned in the Paragraph menu's Spacing dialog box).

By using **Custom** you can provide a value for Custom Width and set the box width independent of other settings. Then, optionally, you can provide a value for Custom Indent. This value will offset the left edge of the box in from the left edge of the paragraph. To create an outdented box instead, use the **Minus** button (see Figure 3).

TIP

If a boxed paragraph begins in one column and continues in another, Ventura will place a box around only the first part of the paragraph. To prevent such a paragraph from splitting, use the Paragraph menu's Breaks dialog box and set **Allow Within** to **No**.

UNDO

With the paragraph selected, use the Paragraph menu and choose **Ruling Box Around**. For Width, select **None** and give the OK.

SEE ALSO

Tags; Breaking Paragraphs

By setting Width to Custom, you can provide a value for Custom Width and set the box width exactly. Then, optionally, you can provide a value for Custom Indent. This value will offset the left edge of the box in from the left edge of the paragraph. To create an outdented box instead, click the Minus (–) button.

Indented box:
Paragraph menu
Ruling Box Around
Custom Indent: 2.3 inches,
Custom Width: .5 inches

By setting Width to Custom, you can provide a value for Custom Width and set the box width exactly. Then, optionally, you can provide a value for Custom Indent. This value will offset the left edge of the box in from the left edge of the paragraph. To create an outdented box instead, click the Minus (–) button.

Outdented box:
Paragraph menu
Ruling Box Around
Custom Indent: –.6 inches,
Custom Width: .5 inches

Figure 3: Custom ruling boxes with paragraph tags

Graphics Boxes

SEQUENCE OF STEPS

Frame mode or also (2.0 only) **Graphics** mode
[select associated frame]
Graphics mode
[click appropriate icon]
[drag mouse to draw graphic]

USAGE

Use the Graphics mode to draw boxes in a more free-form manner. In Frame mode or, with version 2.0, Graphics mode, click the frame that you want the box to be tied to. Then switch to Graphics mode if necessary. Click the Rectangle icon:

to create a standard box or the Rounded Rectangle icon:

to create one with rounded corners or the Box Text icon:

to create a box into which you can insert text. Then, drag the mouse in the working area to create the box. You can then set the attributes for the box (see **Graphics**).

UNDO

In the Graphics mode, select the box. Then press the Delete key or use the Edit menu and choose **Cut Graphic**.

SEE ALSO

Graphics

Box Character

VERSION

2.0 only

SEQUENCE OF STEPS

Text mode
[click location in text]
Edit menu/**Ins Special Item** or **Ctrl-C**
Box Char or **F1**
Hollow (or ↵) or **Filled**

USAGE

Use this procedure to create a box character in the same size as the font you're using. Most fonts do not include such a character. You can use the box character as a check box or a square bullet. It can be hollow (□) or filled (■).

In text mode, position the text cursor where you want to place the box character. Use the Edit menu to choose **Ins Special Item** (or simply press **Ctrl-C**). In the menu that appears, click **Box Char** or press the **F1** key. In the next menu, click **Hollow** or press ↵ and Ventura will insert a hollow (outlined) box; click Filled and Ventura will insert a filled (solid) box at the location of the cursor.

To change the size or color of the box character, or kern it or shift it up or down, use the Edit mode to select the box character by dragging the mouse over it. (When you select a filled black box like this, it will turn white and seem to disappear.) Then use the Side-bar's Set Font button to set text attributes (see **Text**).

UNDO

To remove a box character from text, select the box by positioning the text cursor to the left of it. The words *Box Character* should appear in the Current box. Press the Delete key to remove the box. If desired, you can then paste the box character elsewhere in text (see **Cut/Copy/Paste**).

SEE ALSO

Cut/Copy/Paste; **Text**

Breaking Paragraphs

Defining breaks determines the manner in which one paragraph ends and the next begins.

VERSION

2.0, 1.0, 1.0

SEQUENCE OF STEPS

Paragraph mode
[select a paragraph]
Paragraph menu
Breaks
[set break configuration]
OK or ↵
[tag other paragraphs if desired]

USAGE

The settings for a tag's paragraph break regulate the action that Ventura takes when it encounters paragraphs so tagged. Normally, each paragraph begins on a new line. However, you can set a tag to cause paragraphs not to begin on a new line, or to begin at the top of a new column, or on a new page.

To determine how a paragraph breaks, use the Paragraph mode and select a paragraph. Use the Paragraph menu to choose **Breaks**. In the dialog box are numerous combinations of settings you can adjust before giving the OK.

Paragraphs tagged for Page Break: **Before** will begin on a new page, even if this means that some blank space is left at the bottom of the previous page. Tags for chapter headings often use this setting. Paragraphs tagged for Page Break: **After** will be the last text on the page; text that follows such paragraphs will appear on the next page. Paragraphs with Page Break set to **Before & After** will appear on a separate page; previous text will always appear on the previous page, following text will appear on the next page. Paragraphs tagged with **Before/Until Left** and **Before/Until Right** will begin on a new left and new right page respectively, even if this means a complete blank page or more must precede them to do so.

Paragraphs set for Column Break operate in a fashion similar to those for Page Break. Paragraphs tagged Column Break: **Before** always begin at the top of a new column, even though this may create blank space at the bottom of the previous column.

The usual Line Break setting for paragraphs is **Before**, which causes each paragraph to begin on a new line. You can create multitag paragraphs by adjusting the Line Break setting in conjunction with other settings. This ability is useful for creating *lead-ins*, text at the beginning of a paragraph that is set in a different font from text in the same paragraph that follows it. The effects of Line Breaks are summarized in this chart:

FIRST PARAGRAPH	SECOND PARAGRAPH	SECOND PARAGRAPH ON NEW LINE?
Before	Before	Yes
Before	After	No
Before	Before & After	Yes
After	(All)	Yes
Before & After	(All)	Yes

To create a multitag paragraph, you must also change the second paragraph's Next Y Position to **Beside Last Line Of Prev Para**. In addition, for the second paragraph, you must use the Paragraph menu's Alignment dialog box and set Relative Indent: **On** (see Figure 4).

To keep all the text that comprises a paragraph (such as a table) together on the same page or in the same column, set Allow Within to **No**. To always keep a paragraph (such as a heading) with the paragraph that follows it, set Keep With Next to **Yes**.

UNDO

With the paragraph selected, use the Paragraph menu and choose **Breaks**. The standard settings are Page Break: No,

This is the first paragraph. It is to act as a lead-in to the second paragraph.
This is the second paragraph. Once these paragraphs are joined, they will appear to be one conventional paragraph, governed by two tags, making them one multitag paragraph.

Step 1: Normal settings, both paragraphs. Paragraph menu, Breaks dialog box, Line Break: **Before**.

This is the first paragraph. It is to act as a lead-in to the second paragraph.
This is the second paragraph. Once these paragraphs are joined, they will appear to be one conventional paragraph, governed by two tags, making them one multitag paragraph.

Step 2: Second paragraph: Paragraph menu, Alignment dialog box, Relative Indent: **On**.

This is the first paragraph. It is to act as a lead-in to the second paragraph. This is the second paragraph. Once these paragraphs are joined, they will appear to be one conventional paragraph, governed by two tags, making them one multitag paragraph.

Step 3: Second paragraph: Paragraph menu, Breaks dialog box, Line Break: **No** or **After**; Next Y Position: **Beside Last Line of Prev Para**

Figure 4: Creating a Multitag Paragraph

Column Break: No, Line Break: Before, Next Y Position: Normal, Allow Within: Yes, and Keep With Next: No.

SEE ALSO

Tables; Tags

Bullets

You can place a bullet before all paragraphs assigned a particular tag.

VERSION

2.0, 1.1, 1.0

SEQUENCE OF STEPS

Paragraph mode
[select a paragraph]
Paragraph menu
Special Effects
Special Effect: **Bullet**
[provide a value for Indent After Bullet]
[change other bullet settings if desired]
OK or ↵
[tag other paragraphs if desired]

USAGE

- A bullet is a character, usually a dot, at the beginning of a paragraph. This paragraph has a bullet.

Bullets are often used to set off items in a list. You set this effect by the tag; activating it affects all paragraphs similarly tagged.

To create bulleted paragraphs in a document, take the following steps: in Paragraph mode, select a sample paragraph for the bullet by clicking it with the mouse. Use the Paragraph menu and choose **Special Effects** and then **Bullet**. You must also provide a value for Indent After Bullet, which will determine the amount of additional indent that the main body of text has beyond the bullet.

In the Special Effects dialog box, you can also select one of the characters in the Show Bullet As grouping. By selecting Other, you can provide the ASCII code for any character in the Bullet Char field (see Appendix C).

From the Special Effects dialog box, you can adjust the font Ventura uses for the bullet character you select. Select Commands: **Set Font Properties** and a font dialog box will appear. Use it to adjust the Face, Size, Style (italic, bold), color or Shift up or down (superscript, subscript). Give the OK to return to the Special Effects dialog box. Then click **OK** or press ↵ again.

UNDO

With the paragraph selected, use the Paragraph menu and choose **Special Effects**. Click **None** and give the OK.

SEE ALSO

Fonts; Tags

Capital Letters

You can change text already entered to uppercase or to initial (first letter of each word) capitals.

VERSION

2.0, 1.1, 1.0

SEQUENCE OF STEPS

Text mode
[select text]
Assignment list: **Capitalize** or **Upper Case**

USAGE

To capitalize text after entering it, in Text mode use the mouse to select the text you want to change. Using the Assignment list on the Side-bar, click **Upper Case** to change each character selected to its uppercase equivalent.

To change the selected text to initial capitals, scroll the Assignment list down by clicking the shaded area to its left. Then click **Capitalize**.

Since using Capitalize capitalizes the first letter of each word selected, including those where capitalization is not desirable (for example, prepositions, articles, and conjunctions), you may need to make adjustments by editing individual letters after making the assignment. For this reason, Capitalize works best with those kinds of display type where strict adherence to initial caps is desired for design consideration.

UNDO

With the text selected, click **Lower Case** at the bottom of the Assignment list. You may need to scroll the Assignment list down to reveal this item. Since this procedure changes all characters to lowercase, including those where it may not be proper to do so (such as the first letter in a sentence), you may need to edit individual letters afterward.

Captions

Ventura allows you to add captions to illustrations, number them automatically, add text, make other adjustments, and tag the captions.

VERSION

2.0, 1.1, 1.0

USAGE

You can create captions that are associated with a picture frame by having Ventura generate a special caption frame. You can have Ventura place the caption frame on any side of the picture frame. Once you create a caption frame, the caption frame will remain with its host frame no matter where you move either frame.

You can adjust the caption frame just as you would other frames. By doing so, you can adjust the number of text lines that the caption frame can hold. In Frame mode, select the caption frame and use the frame's handles or the dialog boxes available from the Frame menu (see **Frames**).

You can include an automatic counter for the caption frame. This is a figure or table number that changes automatically as you add or remove captions. Ventura allows you to adjust the number and use various numbering/lettering systems for the caption.

Adding Captions with Automatic Figure Numbers

SEQUENCE OF STEPS

Frame mode
[select the frame]
Frame menu or also (2.0 only) **Graphics** mode
Anchors & Captions
[set caption location and provide a label]
OK or
[add free-form caption if desired]

USAGE

With the **Frame** mode active, select the frame containing the picture or text you want to caption by clicking the frame with your mouse. Then use the **Frame** menu and choose **Anchors & Captions**.

In the Anchors & Captions dialog box, there are five alternatives for Caption: Off, Above, Below, Left, and Right, with Off initially selected. Use one of the other settings both to turn the effect on and to set the location of the caption frame with respect to the host frame.

In the same dialog box, once you set the caption location, you can provide the text of the caption, which Ventura calls its *label*. The label is normally limited to one line (see the section "Free-form Captions" in this entry if you need more than one line) and usually begins with the word *Figure* or *Table* and the corresponding number. Although this text appears within the caption frame, you can edit it only in the dialog box, not within the frame itself. For this reason, some people use free-form captions to create caption text that is easier to edit.

For example, you can type the word *Figure* and then click the button labeled **Figure #**, which creates automatic figure numbers. Clicking this button adds the [F#] code to the label line. You could type in the code yourself, rather than using the button.

You can also use the Table # button to assign the [T#] code, which counts table numbers separately from figure numbers, or you can enter a [C#] code, by clicking **Chapter #**, to use the chapter number as part of the caption. Setting and adjusting these numbers is discussed under **Numbering (Counter) Adjustments**.

With the Text Attr button, you'll make the <D> code appear, Ventura's code for normal text. You can replace the D with a character or text code (see Appendix C) to insert special characters or set text attributes as you would with a word processor.

UNDO

With the host frame or caption frame selected, use the Frame menu and choose **Anchors & Captions**. Set Caption: **Off** to eliminate the caption entirely.

EXAMPLE

<195> Table [C#]-[T#]: <I>This is in italics.

would produce the following for the first table in Chapter 1:

- Table 1-1: *This is in italics.*

SEE ALSO

Frames; Numbering (Counter) Adjustments; Pictures; Text

Free-form Captions

SEQUENCE OF STEPS

Text mode
[insert text cursor in the caption frame]
[add text]

USAGE

Use this technique to add additional text to a caption if the one-line caption label is not sufficient. Free-form captions cannot use automatic counters. However, you can use automatic counters in a caption label and augment them with a free-form caption when necessary.

After you have created a caption, look for the square-shaped end mark (□) within the caption frame. Then, in the text mode, place the text cursor before the end mark and enter as much text as you desire. (You can increase the size of the caption frame if necessary.) If you can't find the end mark, it may be that tabs and returns are hidden or that the caption frame is not big enough. Use the Options menu and choose **Show Tabs and Returns** (or press **Ctrl-T**) or select the frame and enlarge it with its handles.

UNDO

In Text mode, you can edit free-form captions in a caption frame just as you would any standard text.

SEE ALSO

Cut/Copy/Paste; Text

Caption Tags

When you create caption labels and free-form captions, Ventura assigns generated tags to them. You can change the attributes of these tags just as you would any other tag, to change font size, alignment, line spacing, breaks, tabs, and so on. Activate the Paragraph mode, click a sample paragraph, and follow the appropriate sequence of steps to set or change the desired attributes.

Here are the generated tags Ventura assigns to captions:

Z_CAPTION	Free-form captions (created in Text mode).
Z_LABEL CAP	Caption labels with no automatic number.
Z_LABEL TBL	Caption labels with a table number.
Z_LABEL FIG	Caption labels with a figure number.

SEE ALSO

Numbering (Counter) Adjustments; Tags

Centering

See **Alignment**.

Chapters

You can use Ventura's chapter files to coordinate the components of a document, including text, picture, caption, style sheet, and width table files.

VERSION

2.0, 1.1, 1.0

USAGE

Ventura uses chapter files to coordinate other files that make up a document—text, picture, caption, style sheet, and width table files—that is, to locate, position, display, and format text and pictures on the screen and in print. In turn, you can coordinate chapter files, if need be, with a publication file (see **Publications**).

Opening a Chapter File

SEQUENCE OF STEPS

File menu
Open Chapter
[click **Save** *or* **Abandon** *if asked]*
[change directory if desired]
[click file name or type it in]
OK or ↵ or second mouse click

or, when loading Ventura

vp *[optional disk drive] [optional path] [chapter file name]*

USAGE

Use this command to retrieve an existing Ventura chapter file from the disk. The chapter file in turn retrieves other files associated with it and displays their contents on the screen. You can then edit the chapter and its associated files. Changes you make to any of these files are not saved until you save the chapter (see below).

The usual method of opening a chapter is to use the File menu and choose **Open Chapter**. If you are working on a chapter file when you start this procedure and have made changes in it that you haven't saved yet, Ventura will display the prompt

STOP
Save or Abandon changes to this chapter?

meaning the chapter you've been working on. Click the **Save** button to save your work. Click **Abandon** to leave the file on the disk as it was when you last saved it. (Of course, if you've never saved the chapter at all, you'll lose it if you choose **Abandon** now.)

Ventura will then display an Item Selector box. Use it to retrieve the chapter file. Normally, chapter files end with the CHP extension, so use ***.CHP** to display only the files with that ending. Use the backup button to change directories and disk drives (see Appendix B). Click the chapter names. Click **OK** or press ↵ or quickly click the chapter name a second time.

You can also load a chapter when you load (start up) Ventura. To do so, after typing VP at the system prompt, and before pressing ↵, type a space, and, optionally, the disk drive, a colon, and the path. Then type the name of the file and press ↵. When loading, Ventura will display error messages if it can't locate any file associated with the chapter. You will have to locate such files and reassign them if you want to use them with the chapter (see **Text/Picture Files**).

Loading Backup Chapter Files

You can also load the last saved version of the chapter file if, before saving, you've used the Options menu's Set Preferences dialog box and set Keep Backup Files to **Yes**. Backup files substitute the dollar sign for the first character in the extension, and therefore backups for CHP files have the $HP extension. To display only the backup chapter files, use the filter ***.$HP** in the Item Selector box. To display both current and backup chapter files, use ***.?HP**. The Item Selector box will retain the filter you provide until you change it, so remember to switch back to *.CHP when you want to display only current chapter files.

UNDO

If you load a chapter that you don't want, either use the same procedure to open a different file or use File menu/New to start work on a new chapter from scratch.

EXAMPLE

To load Ventura with a file called EXAMPLE that's located on drive C in the SYBEX directory, enter the following in the Item Selector box:

Directory: **C:\SYBEX*.CHP**
Selection: **EXAMPLE.CHP**

Alternatively, you could enter the following at the system prompt:

vp c:\sybex\example

both to start the program and to load the chapter.

SEE ALSO

Publications; Text/Picture Files

Saving a Chapter File

SEQUENCE OF STEPS

File menu
Save
[provide drive, path, and file name if requested]

or

Ctrl-S
[provide drive, path, and file name if requested]

USAGE

Use this procedure either to save a new chapter for the first time or to save the new version of an existing chapter in which you've made changes. Use the File menu and choose **Save** or simply press **Ctrl-S**.

If you are saving a new file, Ventura will display an Item Selector box (see Appendix B). Use it to provide the drive, path, and name for the chapter. Normally, chapter files end with the CHP extension. Although you can edit this extension, it's advisable not to so that you can continue to spot chapter files easily.

With version 2.0, however, if you've loaded a text file into the underlying-page frame (see **Text/Picture Files**), Ventura will not request a chapter name when you save for the first time. Instead, it will automatically assign the same name as the text file to the chapter, but with the CHP extension.

When you save the chapter file, Ventura also saves the changes that you make to other files, including style sheet, text, and caption files. Ventura messages indicate the files that are being saved. It's always best to save as a separate procedure before you quit Ventura (see **Quitting**). Although Ventura will allow you to save when you quit, this technique is not recommended because it could cause you to lose material (with a full disk, for instance).

UNDO

If you realize you shouldn't have saved the changes you made to a chapter, you may be able to retrieve the backup version. You will have a backup version on the disk if you previously used the Options menu's Set Preferences dialog box to set Keep Backup Files to **Yes**.

Use File menu/Open Chapter to open the backup version of the chapter (with the $HP extension), as described above. Then, save the backup, substituting the CHP extension for the $HP extension. Verify that you wish to overwrite the existing CHP file on the disk.

SEE ALSO

Quitting

New Chapter

SEQUENCE OF STEPS

File menu
New
[**Save** (*or* ↵) *or* **Abandon** if prompted]

USAGE

Use this command to clear the screen of a displayed chapter (and its associated text/picture files) so that you can create a new chapter. Ventura will keep the same style sheet, which will be associated with the new chapter unless you load a different style sheet or save the style sheet under a new name (see **Style Sheet**).

If you have a chapter file displayed when you use this command, and you've made changes to it that you haven't saved, Ventura will ask you if you want to save the changes or abandon them. Click **Save** or press ↵ to store the updated chapter on the disk; click **Abandon** to leave the current chapter on the disk as it was.

UNDO

To retrieve the chapter displayed before you used New, use **File** menu/**Open Chapter**, as described above. Open the chapter you had displayed.

Abandoning Chapter Changes

SEQUENCE OF STEPS

File menu
Abandon
[verify with **OK** *or ↵]*

USAGE

To abandon the changes you've made to a chapter file and other files associated with the chapter, use the File menu and choose **Abandon**. Ventura will ask you if you want to abandon the changes you've made to the document and revert to the previously saved version. Choose OK or press ↵ to tell Ventura to go ahead. If you've changed your mind, choose **Cancel**. Once you give the OK, Ventura will reload the chapter from the disk. It will be in the same condition it was when you last saved it.

UNDO

You cannot retrieve edits to a chapter once you've abandoned them, and thus Ventura requests verification before abandoning. Be certain you want to abandon before verifying with

OK. Save your chapter regularly, especially just before you make major changes to it. That way, you can simply abandon the chapter to regain its former condition.

Copying a Chapter File

SEQUENCE OF STEPS

File menu
Save As
[change disk drive and directory if desired]
[provide a new file name]
OK or ↵

USAGE

This procedure copies only the specifications for the chapter file, not other files associated with the chapter, such as text/picture files. To copy all the files associated with a chapter, use **Copy All**, described under **Publications**. **Copy All** also adjusts the pointers that the chapter uses to find files in the correct disk and directory.

Use the **File** menu and select **Save As**. In the Item Selector box that appears, you can change the disk drive and the directory if you wish. Provide a new name for the chapter file and give the OK.

UNDO

Using the File menu, choose **Open Chapter**. Open the chapter under the old name. Use the File menu's DOS File Ops to delete the newly created chapter file.

SEE ALSO

DOS File Operations; Publications

Clipboard

See **Cut /Copy/Paste**.

Color

With a color printer, you can add color to features in all four modes. With version 2.0, you can also define colors by mixing them as you would on a palette and easily separate colors to create overlays.

VERSION

2.0, 1.1, 1.0 (Defining colors and color separations: 2.0 only)

Setting Colors

SEQUENCE OF STEPS

[Activate mode]
[invoke appropriate dialog box]
[choose setting under Color]

USAGE

You can set colors by using text or paragraph fonts, frame backgrounds, and graphic attributes. You can also adjust the color of ruling lines and boxes for both paragraphs and frames.

Table 1 summarizes the methods of setting colors and the scope of each method's effect. For each method, after checking

MODE	MENU	ITEM TO CLICK	COLOR SETTING AFFECTS
Frame	Frame	Frame Background	Space contained by a frame
Graphics	Graphic	Line Attributes	Line or outline of the graphic
Graphics	Graphic	Fill Attributes	Space contained by the graphic
Paragraph	Paragraph	Font	Font of all similarly tagged paragraphs
Text	Side-bar	Set Font button	Font of selected text
Frame or Paragraph	Frame/ Paragraph	Ruling Line or Box	Ruling line/box

Table 1: Methods of setting colors

the appropriate item you'll see a list of the available colors. Choose a color and give the OK.

In any of the dialog boxes, you can use the white setting to create reverse effects. For instance, you can set a frame's background to black and set the font of text within it to white (see **Reverse Type**).

UNDO

Invoke the appropriate dialog box and change the Color setting to Black or another color as desired.

SEE ALSO

Boxes; Fonts; Lines; Reverse Type

Defining Colors

VERSION

2.0 only

SEQUENCE OF STEPS

Paragraph mode
Paragraph menu
Define Colors
[adjust settings]
OK or ↵

USAGE

With release 2.0, you can define the color combinations that Ventura uses as determined by the style sheet. That is, you can redefine all but two of the program's default colors. PostScript printers (QMS Colorscript) can print the resulting customized colors. You can also define shades of gray if you print with a black and white laser printer or typesetter (but the printer may limit you).

When defining a color, you can specify the exact mixture of primary colors that go into making it, and you can provide a name for any color you define. Ventura allows you to redefine its 6 true colors, numbered 2 to 7 (normally Red, Green, Blue, Cyan, Yellow, Magenta). You cannot redefine White (0) or Black (1). Although you can see colors on some color monitors as well as in print, they may differ somewhat when printed, so you should print samples.

To define colors, activate the Paragraph mode and use the Paragraph menu to choose **Define Colors**. The placement of this feature on the Paragraph menu can be misleading, as it affects all colors Ventura uses, not just those associated with paragraphs. For example, when you use the Frame mode and choose the Frame menu's Frame Background dialog box, the colors you defined using the Paragraph menu will appear as options. (If you haven't redefined any colors, the predefined Ventura colors will be listed.)

In the Define Colors dialog box, set Screen Display to **Colors** if you will be using a color printer. Set Screen Display to **Shades of Gray** if you will be using a black and white printer.

Next in the dialog box is the Color Number with arrow buttons on each side. This setting indicates the color number to which the remaining settings in the dialog box apply. By pressing the arrow buttons, you change the number displayed and so display the settings corresponding to that number. You use the next field, Color Setting, in conjunction with color overlays (see below).

Next is the field for Color Name. For Color Number 2, the name *Red* appears. To label more accurately a color that you custom mix, you can edit this field. Eradicate the name that appears there by pressing the Esc key.

Next are four scroll bars that you can use to mix your color. There is one bar for each of Ventura's primary colors, Cyan, Magenta, and Yellow. There is also a scroll bar for Black, which allows you to adjust the color's intensity. If you are defining a shade of gray, set the three colors to 0%, and set Black to the level you desire.

You can set each scroll bar to a value between 0% and 100% in increments of 0.2%. Each time you click one of the arrow buttons on the scroll bar, the value changes by that increment. Each time you click the shadow area of the scroll bar, the value shifts by 10%. You can also slide the white box on a scroll bar to adjust the values by rough amounts. Click **OK** or press ↵ to register your choices.

If a dialog box includes a Pattern setting, set Pattern to **Solid** when you use a custom shade of gray. The Pattern setting can set some shades of gray, but it's recommended that you don't use these two features together.

UNDO

In Paragraph mode, use the Paragraph menu and choose **Define Colors**. Reset the settings to 100% values if desired.

Color Separations

VERSION

2.0 only

SEQUENCE OF STEPS

Paragraph mode
Paragraph menu
Define Color
Color Setting: **Enable** for colors to print,
Disable for colors not to print
File menu
To Print

Spot Color Overlays: **On**
OK or ↵

USAGE

Use this procedure to print in black separate versions of the colors on each page in a document. The pages can then be used with an offset printer to print each color on the pages.

First, in Paragraph mode, use the Paragraph menu to choose **Define Color**. For those colors you will be using, set the Color Setting to **Enable**. Set it to **Disable** for colors you do not use.

When you're ready to print the document, use the File menu to choose **To Print**. In the dialog box, set Spot Color Overlays to **On** and give the OK. Ventura will print each page with the color name and only text set for that color. Not all printers are able to utilize this feature.

UNDO

Use the File menu and choose **To Print**. Set Spot Color Overlays: **Off**.

SEE ALSO

Printing

Inserting Colors with Your Word Processor

USAGE

Use inserted codes to have Ventura assign, as a text attribute, a color that differs from the color assigned by the tag. As such, you use these codes for local font color changes, usually less than one paragraph. For more extensive font colors, assign the color by tag (see **Tags**).

Where the color is to begin, insert the appropriate color number code, **<C0>** through **<C7>,** for the color as defined (see "Defining Colors" above). To reset the font color to that assigned by the tag, use the **<C255>** code. The end of a paragraph (indicated with a return) also resets the font color, as does the appearance of another code.

EXAMPLE

When black is the color of the font that the tag is using, insert the following to change to red and then back to black:

> **This appears in the standard tag color, which is black. <C2>This appears in red. <C255>This is black again.**

SEE ALSO

Font; Text

Columns

You can create newspaper-style columns as a feature of the underlying-page frame or of a standard frame.

VERSION

2.0, 1.1, 1.0

Creating Newspaper-Style Columns

SEQUENCE OF STEPS

Frame mode or also (2.0 only) **Graphics** mode
[select the frame]
Frame menu
Margins & Columns
[click number of columns desired]
[adjust column widths and gutters if desired]
OK or ↵

USAGE

In **Frame** mode, click the standard or underlying-page frame you want to provide with columns. (With version 2.0 you can also use the **Graphics** mode.) Then use the **Frame** menu and choose **Margins & Columns**.

In the dialog box that appears, click a button for the number of columns you want. There are buttons for up to eight columns. Text you assign to the frame will flow into one column after another, automatically. You cannot provide columns for some generated frames (those created by Ventura for headers, footers, and footnotes); but with version 2.0, you can provide columns to frames generated for captions. (You can also use tabs or tags to create columns as part of a table; see **Tables**.)

Initially, Ventura sets up columns of equal width. You can adjust both the width values that appear and the gutters (space between the columns, initially set for zero). As you do, Ventura will tabulate and display the Calculated Width, which is the total of the values you provide for column widths, gutters, and left and right margins. Make sure this value is equal to the value displayed for Actual Frame Width, which is the width of the frame as set with the mouse or with the Frame menu's Sizing & Scaling dialog box.

You can make all columns and all gutters equal. Just provide a value for the first gutter and select Inserts: **Make Equal Widths**.

When the underlying-page frame is set for double-sided pages (as set with the Page Layout dialog box), you can copy this dialog box's settings to the page opposite the one you're working on. Select Inserts: **Copy To Facing Page**.

When you've completed your selections, click **OK** or press ↵.

After creating columns for the underlying-page frame, you can have Ventura indicate the edges of the columns with light dashes. Use the Option menu and choose Show Column Guides. If this option says Hide Column Guides, the column guides are already showing; choose this option to make them disappear.

TIP

To create additional columns for the underlying-page frame beyond the eight columns normally allowed by Ventura, place repeating frames on top of it. Stipulate the multiple columns for the repeating frames with the Frame menu's Margins & Columns dialog box. Assign the same text file to the repeating frames as you do for the underlying-page frame.

UNDO

With the frame selected, use the Frame menu and choose **Margins & Columns**. To remove multiple columns, set # of Columns to 1.

SEE ALSO

Frames; Margins; Options; Tables

Banner Headlines Across Columns

SEQUENCE OF STEPS

Paragraph mode
[select the headline paragraph]
Paragraph menu
(2.0): **Attribute Overrides;** (1.1,1.0): **Alignment**
Line Width: **Frame-Wide**
OK or ↵

USAGE

Normally, headlines appear above the text in one column only. To cause text to stretch across all the columns in a frame, making a banner headline, you can create a paragraph tag with a frame-wide status.

In Paragraph mode, click a sample headline. Pull down the Paragraph menu and select **Attribute Overrides** (before 2.0, select **Alignment**). For Line Width, choose **Frame-Wide** and give the OK. All similarly tagged paragraphs will receive the same effect.

UNDO

With the headline paragraph selected, pull down the Paragraph menu and choose **Alignment**. Change Line Width to **Column-Wide** and give the OK.

Balancing Columns

SEQUENCE OF STEPS

Frame mode or also (2.0 only) **Graphics** mode
[select the frame]
Frame menu
(2.0) **Frame Typography;** (1.1, 1.0): **Sizing & Scaling**
Column Balance: **On**
OK or ↵

USAGE

This feature ensures that the text within a multicolumn frame ends evenly at the bottom of each column. In **Frame** mode (or also, with version 2.0, **Graphics** mode), first select the multi-column frame, and then use the **Frame** menu's **Frame Typography** dialog box (**Sizing & Scaling** before version 2.0) to set Column Balance: **On**.

When the columns in such a frame have Frame-Wide headlines (as discussed above), selecting Column Balance On ensures that each column of text will fall under the appropriate headline.

UNDO

With the frame selected, use the Frame menu's Sizing & Scaling dialog box to set Column Balance: **Off**.

SEE ALSO

Frames

Copying

Copying a chapter file only, see **Chapters.**
Copying a chapter and associated files, see **Publications.**
Copying publications, see **Publications.**
Copying style sheets, see **Style Sheets.**
Copying text files, see **Text/Picture Files.**
Copying text, frames, graphics, see **Cut/Copy/Paste.**

Cut/Copy/Paste

You use cut, copy, and paste procedures to manipulate frames, text, or graphics, each in its respective mode.

VERSION

2.0, 1.1, and 1.0

USAGE

To effect these operations, you can use the Edit menu or the Delete and Insert keys. These procedures use the clipboard, an unseen area of Ventura that you can cut or copy material to. *Cutting* material removes it from its original location and places it on the clipboard. *Copying* leaves material in place, making a copy of it for the clipboard. There are actually three clipboards, one each for frames, text, and graphics. Newly cut or copied material replaces material on the corresponding clipboard; if it was cut and not pasted somewhere else, that material is permanently deleted.

By *pasting*, you insert material from the clipboard into the chapter. Thus, you can cut and paste to effect a move or simply cut to delete unwanted material. After pasting, the material also remains on the clipboard, which means you can paste it elsewhere as well, if desired.

Because material remains on the clipboard until you replace it—even if you load a different chapter, abandon the current version of the chapter, or clear the Ventura screen to work on a brand new chapter—you can use the clipboard to move material from one chapter to another. Ventura clears the clipboard when you quit the program.

When you cut, copy, or paste a frame, you also cut, copy, and paste any graphics that you've tied to the frame (see **Graphics**).

Cutting Frames, Text, Graphics

SEQUENCE OF STEPS

Frame mode, **Text** mode, or **Graphics** mode
[select corresponding material]
Edit menu/**Cut Frame**, **Cut Text**, or **Cut Graphic**
or **Delete** key

USAGE

To cut material, first use the appropriate mode to select the material.

Cutting Text To cut text, activate the Text mode and select the text with the mouse (see **Text**). You can select and cut only one continuous length of text to the clipboard. To delete the selected text, press the Delete key or use Edit menu/**Cut Text**.

Ventura will delete the text from the screen and place it on the text clipboard.

Note that text attributes assigned with the Text mode's Assignment list (such as superscript, underline, and strike-thru) remain with text that is cut. Tag assignments remain only when the Paragraph mark at the end of the paragraph in question is cut as part of the text.

Cutting Frames and Graphics To cut a frame, activate the Frame mode and select the frame by clicking it. To cut a graphic, activate the Graphics mode and select the graphic by clicking it. (To cut a graphic before version 2.0, you must begin by activating the Frame mode and selecting the associated frame. Then use the Graphics mode to select the graphic.)

You can use the Shift key to select multiple frames or graphics to cut simultaneously. All such multiple items are placed on the clipboard as a unit.

Once you've selected your material, press the Delete key or use Edit menu/**Cut**. (The Edit menu will read Cut Frame or Cut Graphic, as dictated by Ventura's current mode.) The material will disappear from the screen, and Ventura will place it on the clipboard.

UNDO

To retrieve material inadvertently cut to the clipboard, immediately use the paste procedure described below to insert it back, before cutting similar material. Material on the clipboard that's replaced with new material cannot be retrieved.

SEE ALSO

Frames; Graphics; Text

Copying Frames, Text, Graphics

SEQUENCE OF STEPS

Frame mode, **Text** mode, or **Graphics** mode
[select corresponding material]
Edit menu/**Copy Frame**, **Copy Text**, or **Copy Graphic**
or
Shift-Delete

USAGE

Use Copying to make a copy of material from the current chapter onto the clipboard. You then paste the clipboard material elsewhere, thus copying it from one place to another.

To copy material, first use the appropriate mode to select the material. Use the same techniques as described under "Cutting Frames, Text, Graphics," above. Once you've selected your material, press Shift-Delete or use Edit menu/**Copy**. (The Edit menu will appear as Copy Frame, Copy Text, or Copy Graphic, as dictated by Ventura's current mode.) The material will remain on the screen (although you may see it "blink"), but Ventura will place a copy of it on the clipboard.

TIP

When copying frames and graphics, Ventura takes note of the position they occupy on the page; if they are later pasted, Ventura inserts them into the same position on the page.

Frame text and box text will copy along with the frame or graphic they correspond to. If a frame is assigned a text/picture file, the copy will be assigned the same file (see **Text/Picture Files**). All attributes of the frame or graphic will be copied as well, such as margins, ruling lines, and background.

UNDO

Since copying to the clipboard does not affect the material in the displayed chapter, there is no alteration to undo. Material on the clipboard that's replaced with new material cannot be retrieved.

SEE ALSO

Frames; Graphics; Text; Text/Picture Files

Pasting Frames, Text, Graphics

SEQUENCE OF STEPS

Frame mode, **Text** mode, or **Graphics** mode
[select page or text position]
Edit menu/**Paste Frame**, **Paste Text**, or **Paste Graphic**
or
Insert key

USAGE

Use Pasting to insert a copy of material that's on the clipboard into the document. To paste text, use the mouse to place the text cursor where you want the text to appear. To paste frames or graphics, go to the page where you want the frame(s) or graphic(s) to appear. Once you have the proper location, press the Insert key or use the Edit menu's **Paste** command. (The menu will appear as Paste Frame, Paste Text, or Paste Graphic, depending on the current mode.) This will cause the corresponding material on the clipboard to appear within the document. If you've cut or copied multiple frames or graphics to the clipboard, pasting places them all in place at once.

When you paste, the material also remains on the clipboard, and you can paste it again elsewhere, if necessary. You can use this ability to insert boilerplate text in more than one location or to use a graphic repeatedly. You can also make copies of frames, which is useful if you want to create new frames that share attributes (such as background and ruling box) of an existing frame. Because the clipboard isn't cleared when you open a new chapter, you can copy material from chapter to chapter.

Pasting Frames When you paste a frame, Ventura will place it in the same position on the page that it occupied when you cut or copied it. Therefore, if you plan to copy a frame to the clipboard and then paste a copy of it back on the same page (to create a new frame sharing size and other attributes), move the original frame away with the mouse after you copy and before you paste. Otherwise, you'll end up with two identical frames, exactly on top of one another. You may not even realize that the copy has been pasted. If you do, however, you can click the frame on top of the pile to move it off the other frame. You can also use Ctrl-click to select among piled frames.

Frame text that appeared within the frame when it was cut or copied will appear in the newly pasted frame as well. Frames assigned a text/picture file before being cut or copied to the clipboard will have the same assignment after being pasted back on the screen even if the document does not have the file on its Frame mode Assignment list; Ventura will load the file and add it to the list if necessary.

Pasting Graphics Before pasting a graphic, select the frame that you want the graphic to be tied to. (Before version 2.0, you must use the Frame mode to do this.) The pasted graphic will be associated with the selected frame, even if it was tied to a different frame when you cut or copied it to the clipboard. If you don't select a frame before switching to the Graphics mode, Ventura will select the underlying-page frame. If no frame is selected (because you changed pages while in the Graphics mode, for instance), you will not be able to paste the graphic on the page.

Like frames, pasted graphics appear in the same position they occupied when cut or copied to the clipboard. Use the same techniques described for frames to deal with identical graphics piled on top of one another.

UNDO

To remove incorrectly pasted material, with the material selected use one of the Cut techniques described above.

Deleting

Deleting (cutting) text, frames, graphics, see **Cut/Copy/Paste**.
Deleting a chapter from a publication, see **Publications**.
Deleting files from disk, see **DOS File Operations**.
Deleting files from frames, see **Text/Picture Files**.
Deleting tags, see **Tags**.

DOS File Operations

Use the DOS File Operations dialog box to manage system operations without leaving Ventura.

VERSION

2.0, 1.1, 1.0

SEQUENCE OF STEPS

(2.0, 1.1) **File** menu or (1.0) **Options** menu
DOS **File Ops**
[click **Select Different File Specification** *or edit* **File Spec** *field if desired]*
Make Directory or **Remove Directory** or **Delete Matching File(s)**

USAGE

Use the DOS File Operations dialog box to remove files from the disk and make directories and remove them. You may need to use this dialog box if Ventura displays a "disk full" message when you save. You can also use it to list files or to create directories so that you can store Ventura files appropriately.

Use the File menu to choose **DOS File Ops.** In the resulting dialog box you'll see a File Spec field that lists a drive, path, and file name and can use wildcard characters (* and ?). The question mark (?) represents a single character, and the asterisk (*) indicates a group of characters. Ventura will use this field as a guide for operations.

You can change the File Spec field by editing it or by choosing the **Select Different File Specification** button, which causes an Item Selector box to appear. By using the **Backup** button and clicking a directory or file name, you can change the file specification without typing it in. Use OK on the Item Selector, and the DOS File Operations dialog box reappears.

You can click the **Make Directory** button to create a directory with the name you provide for File Spec. You must provide a directory name with the keyboard; you cannot use the Item Selector list and the Backup button, because they work only with existing files and directories. For example, to create a SYBEX directory on drive C you would enter

File Spec: **C:\SYBEX**

You can, however, use the Item Selector list to choose a directory to delete. You can also enter the name with the keyboard. Once you have the appropriate File Spec, click the **Remove Directory** button.

Use **Delete Matching File(s)** to delete a single file or a group of files matching the file specification. You can select single files with the Item Selector list, but to indicate a group of files you must enter wildcards with the keyboard.

UNDO

You can remove directories that you've made, and you can again make directories that you've removed. However, you cannot retrieve files that you've deleted. Ventura will ask for verification before deleting numerous files at once.

SEE ALSO

Chapters; Style Sheets; Publications; Text/Picture Files

Edit Menu

Cut/Copy/Paste, see **Cut/Copy/Paste**.
Insert/Edit Special Item, see **Boxes, Footnotes, Indexing, Fractions, Anchoring Frames.**
Remove/Rename files, see **Text/Picture Files.**

File Management

See **DOS File Operations, Chapters, Style Sheets, Publications, Text/Picture Files.**

Fonts

Ventura allows you to assign or change fonts in several ways.

USAGE

A *font* is a complete set of alphanumeric and symbol characters in a specific face, size, and style. Thus, Swiss 10 Bold is a different font from Swiss 10 Normal, which is a different font from Swiss 14 Normal as well.

You can assign a font by tags, to affect all paragraphs so tagged. You can also assign a font to individual characters within a paragraph. You can assign text fonts when entering text with your word processor. You can also assign a font to special features, like big first characters. Use the Set Font Properties command associated with the feature you want.

Assigning Fonts with a Paragraph Tag

VERSION

2.0, 1.1, 1.0

SEQUENCE OF STEPS

Paragraph mode
[select a paragraph]
Paragraph menu
Font
[set the font properties]
OK or ↵
[tag other paragraphs if desired]

USAGE

By assigning a font with a paragraph tag, you set all characters in the selected paragraph (and all similarly tagged paragraphs) in a particular font. However, this method will not affect text that has been assigned a font locally, as a text attribute (see "Assigning Fonts to Selected Text," below).

First activate Paragraph mode and click a sample paragraph whose font you wish to adjust. Then use the Paragraph menu and choose **Font**. In the dialog box that appears (Figure 5), adjust the settings under Face, Size, and Style as desired. The settings you see will depend on the width table you're using (Options menu/Set Printer Info). Note that the availability of some font settings may depend on prior settings in the dialog box.

TIP

As you adjust the size of a font, you can have Ventura adjust the vertical paragraph and line spacing to maintain the same proportion with the new font size. To do so, use the Options menu and choose **Set Preferences**. In the resulting dialog box, with version 2.0 set Auto-Adjustments to Styles. (With version 1.1, set Auto-Adjust Styles to Yes. This feature is not available for 1.0.) The values set with the Paragraph menu's Spacing dialog box for Above, Below, Inter-Line, and Inter-Paragraph will adjust along with the font for the tag. (Auto-Adjustments: Both also activates this feature and causes Ventura to auto-adjust quotes and dashes as well; see **Text**.)

UNDO

With the paragraph tagged, use the Paragraph menu and choose **Font**. Change the settings back and give the OK.

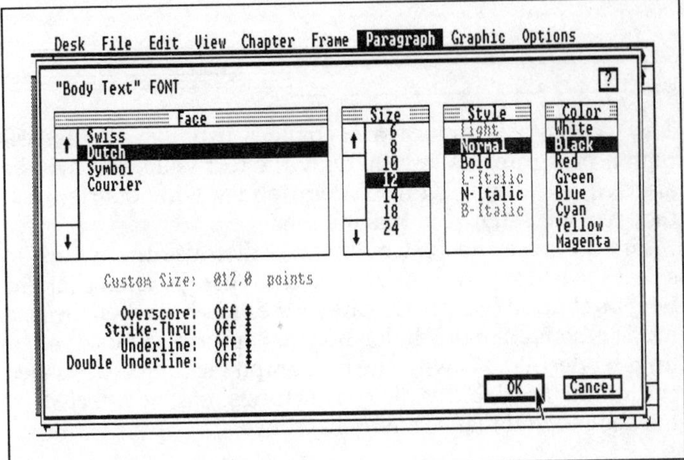

Figure 5: Font dialog box

SEE ALSO

Bold; Italics; Spacing; Tags

Assigning Fonts to Selected Text

VERSION

2.0, 1.1, 1.0

SEQUENCE OF STEPS

Text mode
[select the text]
Side-bar: **Set Font**
[adjust the settings]
OK or ↵

USAGE

This technique is for local font changes, usually with text less than a paragraph in length. Only the text you select will be affected, and changing the paragraph tag will not affect text that you've assigned in this manner.

First activate the Text mode, and then use the mouse to select the text whose font you want to change. Then click the **Set Font** button (which appears on the Side-bar when the Text mode is active). In the dialog box that appears, adjust the settings as desired. As with the paragraph technique described earlier, the availability of some settings may be affected by the choices you make for other settings.

UNDO

If you catch an error while the text is still highlighted, you can simply click **Normal** on the Side-bar to remove the font attributes. The selected text will change to the standard settings that you've assigned for the paragraph. If you have other text attributes that must remain in place, click the **Set Font** button instead. Then adjust the settings to remove what you don't want.

If you don't catch the error while the text is still selected, delete the attribute codes that mark the beginning and end of the font change. In Text mode, use the mouse to place the text cursor at the end of the nonstandard font. Move the text cursor with the ← or → key until the words *Attr. Setting* appear in the Current box. Then press the Delete key to delete the code. Repeat the procedure at the beginning of the text. (You work backward in order to keep from losing the position of the codes as the text changes to normal.)

EXAMPLE

See Figure 6.

SEE ALSO

Bold; Italics; Kerning; Subscript/Superscript; Text

Software Salaries: How do YOU stack up?

Figure 6: Font change within a paragraph

Assigning the Small Attribute

VERSION

2.0, 1.1, 1.0

SEQUENCE OF STEPS

Text mode
[Select the text]
Assignment list: **Small**

USAGE

In Text mode, use the Assignment list's Small attribute to automatically adjust selected text to the next smaller font size. (Custom sizes are adjusted downward by two points.) If you later adjust the size of the font assigned to the paragraph tag, Ventura will automatically adjust text with the Small attribute to the next smaller size of the new font.

TIP

You can easily create small caps out of lowercase text. Select the text, click the Assignment list's **Upper Case** setting, and then click **Small**. Be aware that this procedure will also convert letters that were originally capitals; you may wish then to change such letters back to "normal" capitals.

UNDO

Follow the same techniques described for neutralizing text fonts described above—that is, click **Normal** or delete the Attr Setting codes.

SEE ALSO

Capital Letters; Fonts

Adding Fonts to the Width Table

VERSION

2.0 and 1.1 only

SEQUENCE OF STEPS

[copy the width table in use]
[copy the new font and its width table to the VENTURA directory]
Ventura's **Options** menu
Set Printer Info
Command: **Load Different Width Table**
[load the width table you want to add the font to]
Options menu
Add/Remove Fonts
Command: **Merge Width Tables**
[load the width table of new font]
Command: **Save As New Width Table**
[provide a new name for the width table]

USAGE

To add a font to Ventura, you add the font to an existing width table and save the result as a new width table. Ventura uses width tables to store the size of each character in the fonts. You can acquire fonts and corresponding width tables from third-party vendors.

For safety, begin by using DOS to make a copy of the width table to which you will be adding the fonts. Copy your new font and the width table provided with it to the VENTURA directory. (With PostScript printers, make and use the PSFONTS directory.) Then, in Ventura, use the Options menu and choose **Set Printer Info**. Load the old width table to which you want to add the new font. Then use the Options menu again and choose **Add/Remove Fonts**. In the resulting dialog box, click **Merge Width Tables**. Use the Item Selector box that appears to load the width table of the new font, which will combine the two width tables. Click **Save As New Width Table** and make up a name for the new width table that now contains all the fonts, both old and new. Ventura automatically uses the new width table.

Each font has a download/resident status assigned by Ventura during installation. The status of the indicated font appears at the bottom of the Style column. If you use your printer's software to download fonts to your printer prior to using Ventura, you can change fonts from Download to Resident status. Click the word **Download** to change it to **Resident**.

You can also use this same dialog box to remove a font from a width table. Select the combination of face, size, and style that you want to remove. Then click **Remove Selected Font**. Save this edited width table under the name you desire.

TIP

Since each combination of face, size, and style is a different font, if you want to change each font in a given typeface from Download to Resident, you may need to change the download/resident status of several combinations. Similarly, should you wish to remove all fonts for a particular face, you would have to remove all size/style combinations for that face.

UNDO

Use the Options menu's Set Printer Info dialog box. Load the original width table.

SEE ALSO

Printing

Assigning Text Fonts with Your Word Processor

VERSION

2.0, 1.1, 1.0

SEQUENCE OF STEPS

<[beginning code]>[text]<[ending code]>

USAGE

To use your word processor to assign a font that's set as a text attribute (text font), you place a code at the beginning and end of the text you want to change. Use this technique only for local changes generally no longer than a paragraph. For more general changes, assign the font with a paragraph tag (see **Tags**).

To set a text font with your word processor, you place a code within < > symbols at the beginning of the text to appear in the nonstandard font. Place another code at the end of the nonstandard font to return the text to normal (as set by the paragraph tag) at that point. You can eliminate this ending code if the effect continues to the end of the paragraph, because the effect will end when the paragraph ends unless the code appears again at the beginning of the next paragraph. You can also eliminate it if the effect ends where a new effect begins because a new code cancels previous effects.

The codes you can use appear in Appendix C; some important codes are discussed in the following paragraphs.

Setting the Size of a Text Font To adjust only the size of the font, use the letter P followed by the point size. To return to the point size set by the paragraph's tag, use the <P255> code.

To assign the Small attribute, use the code <S> at the beginning of the small text. Use the code <D> to switch back to the normal tag setting.

Setting the Face of a Text Font To change only the face of the font, use the letter F in conjunction with a code number. Here are the code numbers for some popular faces:

<F1>	Courier
<F2>	Swiss (Helvetica)
<F14>	Dutch (Times)
<F20>	New Century Schoolbook
<F50>	Helvetica Narrow
<F105>	Letter Gothic
<F128>	Symbol
<F255>	Reset to face set by the tag

To find the appropriate number for other faces, create a test document with Ventura, using the Text mode's **Set Font** button to assign the face by name to some text stored in your word processor's format. Then open the text file with your word processor and examine the code at the beginning of the text. You can then use the code you find to assign the same face locally as you desire.

EXAMPLE

This is normal. <P18>This is an 18 point font. <P255>This is normal again. <S>THIS IS SMALL CAPS. <D>This is normal again.

produces the following result when the standard font is 10 points:

This is normal. This is an 18 point font.
This is normal again. THIS IS SMALL CAPS. This is normal again.

Footnotes

To use footnotes, you must first turn on the footnote system. You can then insert footnotes with Ventura. You can also use your word processor to insert footnotes, which will appear in Ventura when the footnote system is on.

VERSION

2.0, 1.1, 1.0

USAGE

You can use footnotes only in text that appears in the underlying-page frame. You cannot provide footnotes for text files assigned to standard frames or to CAP file text (Frame Text, Box Text, and captions).

Turning Footnotes On

SEQUENCE OF STEPS

(2.0) **Chapter** menu or (1.1, 1.0) **Page** menu
Footnote Settings

[set **Usage & Format** *and other settings]*
OK or ↵

USAGE

In the Chapter screen's Footnote Settings dialog box, turn on the footnote system with the Usage & Format grouping. Select some setting other than Off.

The setting you select indicates whether you want to number the footnotes from the start of each page, using automatic numbers or user-defined strings, or from the start of each chapter. User-defined strings are characters you provide in this dialog box as the footnote symbol, such as the asterisk (*).

You also use this dialog box to specify the footnote number with which you want Ventura to begin numbering the chapter. Use the **Start With #** setting to do this.

In the Number Template field you provide a format that Ventura uses for the numbers at the bottom of the page. Insert the # symbol where you want the footnote number to appear. Thus, entering - # - for the number template would produce -1- for the first footnote at the bottom of the page.

You can use the Position Of Number settings to superscript or subscript the footnote number in the text. Doing so automatically decreases the size of the character. This setting does not affect the number at the bottom of the page.

Also use this box to adjust the separator line that appears at the bottom of the page between the document text and the text of the footnote. Separator Line Width is the length of the line from left to right (although Ventura will subtract the left margin of the footnote frame; see "Tip" below). Space Above Line is the distance between the document's text area and the line. Height Of Line is for the thickness of the line from top to bottom.

UNDO

Using the same dialog box, set Usage & Format to **Off** to disengage the footnote system.

Inserting Footnotes with Ventura

SEQUENCE OF STEPS

Text mode
[position keyboard cursor in the text]
Edit menu
(2.0 only) **Ins Special Item** or **Ctrl-C**
(2.0) **Footnote** or **F2**; (1.1 and 1.0) **Insert Footnote**
[edit text of footnote at the bottom of the page]

USAGE

In the text mode, position the keyboard cursor at the spot in the text where you want the automatic number or other footnote mark to appear. The footnote number or user-defined string that you specified in the Footnote Settings dialog box (described above) will appear at that spot. If tabs and returns are showing (see **Options**), you'll also see a degree symbol (°) appear.

Simultaneously, at the bottom of the page, you'll see a duplicate of the automatic number or other footnote mark, along with the words *Text of Footnote,* appear within a generated frame. Delete these words and insert the text of your actual footnote.

TIP

You can adjust both the format and the positioning of footnotes at the bottom of the page. Ventura automatically assigns the generated tag Z_FNOT ENTRY to the "Text of Footnote" paragraph at the bottom of the page and the Z_FNOT # tag to the accompanying automatic number or other reference mark. By using the Paragraph mode to click either of these paragraphs, you can adjust its tag settings with the Paragraph menu to control Font, Alignment, Spacing, Breaks, and so on.

(To assign attributes to footnote numbers/marks that appear within the document's text, you must use the Footnotes Settings dialog box as described above.)

In addition, by using the Frame mode, you can click the footnote's generated frame to adjust some aspects of the frame. With the Frame's menus Margins & Columns dialog box, you can adjust the margins of the frame. Decreasing the margins decreases the size of the frame. Ventura will subtract the value of the frame's left margin from the Separator Line Width; you can increase the Separator Line Width by the same amount to compensate. You cannot make adjustments to the column settings.

UNDO

To remove a particular footnote, place the keyboard cursor to the left of the footnote number or other mark. Then press the Delete key to delete it and its corresponding footnote text. (The text goes to the clipboard; you can insert it elsewhere in your document.)

SEE ALSO

Cut/Copy/Paste; Frames; Tags

Inserting Footnotes with Your Word Processor

SEQUENCE OF STEPS

<$F*[text of footnote]***>**

USAGE

Decide where you want a footnote number or other reference mark to appear. Then, in your word-processed text file, enter the left angle bracket (<) followed by a dollar sign and the letter F. Enter the text of your footnote, ending with the right angle bracket (>). In Ventura, the text will appear at the bottom of the page.

UNDO

Use your word processor's delete or undo capabilities to remove the codes and, if desired, the text as well. You can also use Ventura to remove the footnote, as described above.

EXAMPLE

> I want a footnote number to appear at the end of this sentence.<$FThis is the number's corresponding footnote text, for the bottom of the page.> Here the document continues.

would print as

> I want a footnote number to appear at the end of this sentence.[1] Here the document continues.
>
> ---
>
> 1 This is the number's corresponding footnote text, for the bottom of the page.

SEE ALSO

Text

Fractions

You can insert true fractions into a text or edit existing ones.

VERSION

2.0 only

SEQUENCE OF STEPS

To insert a fraction into the text:

Text mode
[position the keyboard cursor in the text]
Edit menu
Ins Special Item or **Ctrl-C**
Fraction or **F4**
[type the fraction, entering **Ctrl-C F1** *for slash (/) or* **Ctrl-C F2** *for over (–)]*
[type **Ctrl-D** *when done]*

To edit an existing fraction in the text:

Text mode
[position the keyboard cursor before the fraction]
Edit menu
Edit Special Item or **Ctrl-D**

[edit fraction, entering **Ctrl-C F1** *for slash (/) or* **Ctrl-C F2** *for over (–)]*
[type **Ctrl-D** *when done]*

USAGE

This procedure lets you easily enter typographically correct fractions into a document. Ventura automatically uses a font smaller than the tag stipulates. You can create two types of fractions: those that use a slash ($^1/_2$) or those that use an "over" bar ($\frac{1}{2}$).

To insert the fraction, activate the text mode and place the keyboard cursor in the text where you want the fraction to appear. Then type **Ctrl-C** or use the Edit menu and choose **Ins Special Item**. From the menu that appears, click **Fraction** or press **F4**. The screen will divide into two sections—an upper section with a cursor and a blank lower section. Type your fraction into the upper section, and when it comes time for the division mark, press **Ctrl-C**. A menu will appear prompting you to specify the type of division mark:

fraction (/)	F1
over (-)	F2

Press the appropriate Function key and, after a moment, your results will appear in the lower portion of the screen. Finish typing the fraction, and then press **Ctrl-D**. Ventura will redisplay your document in the working area with the fraction in place.

To edit an existing fraction, place the keyboard cursor to its left. The word *Fraction* should appear in the Current box toward the bottom of the Side-bar. Type **Ctrl-D** or use the Edit menu and choose **Edit Special Item**. The fraction split screen will appear; edit the fraction and type **Ctrl-D** when you're done.

UNDO

To remove a fraction, use Text mode to position the keyboard cursor to the left of the fraction. The word *Fraction* should appear in the Current box. Then press the Delete key. (You can use this technique to move a fraction to another location; see **Cut/Copy/Paste**.)

EXAMPLE

To enter three-fourths, you'd enter the following into the top part of the fraction split screen:

3
Ctrl-C
F1 for slash (/) or **F2** for over (–)
4
Ctrl-D

which would display as $^3/_4$ or $(\frac{3}{4})$, depending on the division mark you specify.

Frames

Frames are Ventura's containers for holding text and pictures.

VERSION

2.0, 1.1, 1.0

USAGE

To work with frames, you first activate the Frame mode. (With version 2.0, you can also use the Graphics mode for some procedures.) Then you use the mouse to create a frame or to select an existing frame that you want to adjust. Once you select a frame, you can place it on the page, align the frame with text and in columns, and change the size of the frame. You can have text flow around the frame automatically (or allow it to bleed through) or create a "padded" area around the frame that's free of text. You can also make the frame appear repeatedly on page after page. Normally, frames are invisible when you print the document. If desired, however, you can outline the frame with up to three lines, either within the periphery of the frame or only at the top or bottom of the frame. You can also shade the frame's background.

This section examines the features and procedures listed above. However, frames are a fundamental concept within Ventura, affecting many of its features, and many aspects of frames are discussed elsewhere in this book. **Columns** and **Margins** are each listed separately, describing how you can create these within a frame. To remove a frame from the page or to move or copy it to a different page, see **Cut/Copy/Paste**. See **Ruler** for information on using this feature with frames.

To use a word-processed file or an imported picture, you load it and assign its file to a frame. To understand how to perform this and related procedures, see **Text/Picture Files**.

To manipulate pictures as they appear in a frame, see **Pictures**. To see how to create a frame that holds the caption of a picture, see **Captions**. To understand how to tie a picture frame to a specific spot in the text, see **Anchoring Frames**.

To adjust the color of a frame, see **Color**. See **Reverse Type** for information on this and related effects, which you can accomplish by changing the background of a frame.

You tie Ventura's graphics to a frame (see **Graphics**) and you can run boxes or lines around frames (see **Boxes** and **Line Drawing**).

Underlying-Page Frame

The underlying-page frame is a special kind of frame different from other (standard) frames. Generally, this frame is the same size as the page, and you use it to set up some of the internal parameters of the page, like margins. Every Ventura document has at least one underlying-page frame, automatically created. The underlying-page frame is always at the back (on the bottom) of any pile of frames; you place other frames in front (on top) of it. Most documents have only one underlying-page frame to ensure that each page is similar in appearance. However, you can insert a different underlying-page frame if you want to change the page layout at some point in the document. For a discussion of how to do this, see **Page Formats**.

Generated Frames

When you use some features, Ventura creates a *generated* frame automatically. With these frames you are more restricted in the operations you can perform than with other frames. See **Captions**, **Footnotes**, and **Headers/Footers** for discussions on how to work with the generated frames these features create.

Activating Frame Mode

SEQUENCE OF STEPS

Frame button or **View** menu/**Frame Setting** or **Ctrl-U**

USAGE

Generally, you activate the Frame mode to create a frame or perform an operation on one. (With version 2.0, you can also perform some frame operations in the Graphics mode, making it easier to work with graphics; see **Graphics**).

You can use any of three methods to activate the Frame mode. You can click the **Frame** button, which is the first of four buttons at the top of the Side-bar; you can pull down the View menu and choose **Frame setting**; or you can press **Ctrl-U** on the keyboard.

UNDO

Use one of the methods for switching Ventura to one of its other modes (Paragraph, Text, or Graphics mode).

EXAMPLE

See Figure 7.

SEE ALSO

Graphics; Side-bar; Tags; Text

USING THE SIDE-BAR	USING THE VIEW MENU	USING THE KEYBOARD	RESULTING MOUSE SHAPE
 Text	 View Facing Pages View Reduced View ^R √ Normal View (1x) ^N Enlarged View (2x) ^E √ Frame Setting ^U Paragraph Tagging ^I Text Editing ^O Graphic Drawing ^P	 CTRL - U	 +

Figure 7: Activating Frame mode

Creating Frames

SEQUENCE OF STEPS

Frame mode or also (2.0 only) **Graphics** mode
Add New Frame button
[position mouse in top-left corner for the frame]
[drag mouse to bottom-right corner for the frame]
[release the mouse]

USAGE

In Frame mode, click the **Add New Frame** button that appears at the top of the Side-bar. (With version 2.0, you can also use the Graphics mode.) Move the mouse/cursor to where you want the top-left corner of the frame to be located. As you do, the mouse cursor will change to a corner bracket enclosing the letters FR, as shown in Figure 8(a). Press and hold the mouse while you head toward the bottom-left corner you want for the frame. The mouse cursor changes to a flattened hand as shown in Figure 8(b). Release the mouse at the bottom-right corner, which establishes the new frame. The mouse cursor changes to the shape of a plus sign.

Once you create a new frame, it is automatically selected. This is indicated on the screen by the black handles that appear along its edges.

The newly created frame has no file or text assigned to it. This is indicated by the word *Empty* that appears in the Current box after you create the frame (or should you select the frame again later). For the contents of a text or picture file to appear in the frame, you must load the file and assign it to the frame (see **Text/Picture Files**). Alternatively, you can enter Frame Text directly into the frame, which is assigned to the chapter's CAP file (see **Text**).

To create multiple frames, hold down the Shift key as you create each frame. The Add New Frame button remains selected and the mouse cursor returns to the bracketed-FR shape after each frame. Release the Shift key before creating the final frame.

UNDO

To remove a newly created frame, simply cut the selected frame by pressing the Delete key (see **Cut/Copy/Paste**).

EXAMPLE

See Figure 8.

SEE ALSO

Cut/Copy/Paste; Text; Text/Picture Files

Selecting Frames

SEQUENCE OF STEPS

Frame mode or also (2.0 only) **Graphics** mode
[position the mouse within the frame]
[click the mouse]

USAGE

Select a frame when you want to work with it. Activate the Frame mode (or Graphics mode in 2.0). Then position the mouse cursor some where within the frame that you want to select and click. This action selects the frame, as indicated by the eight black handles that appear along the periphery of the frame (see Figure 9). Smaller frames will have fewer selection handles.

Once a frame is selected, the Current box indicates the contents of the frame. It will display the name of the text/picture file assigned to the frame, or *Frame Text* if text is entered directly into the frame. The word *Empty* appears if nothing is assigned to the frame. Generated frames will display *Caption, Footnote,* or, depending on the side of a double-sided page, *L. Header, R. Header, L. Footer,* or *R. Footer.*

Newly created and newly pasted (see **Cut/Copy/Paste**) frames are automatically selected.

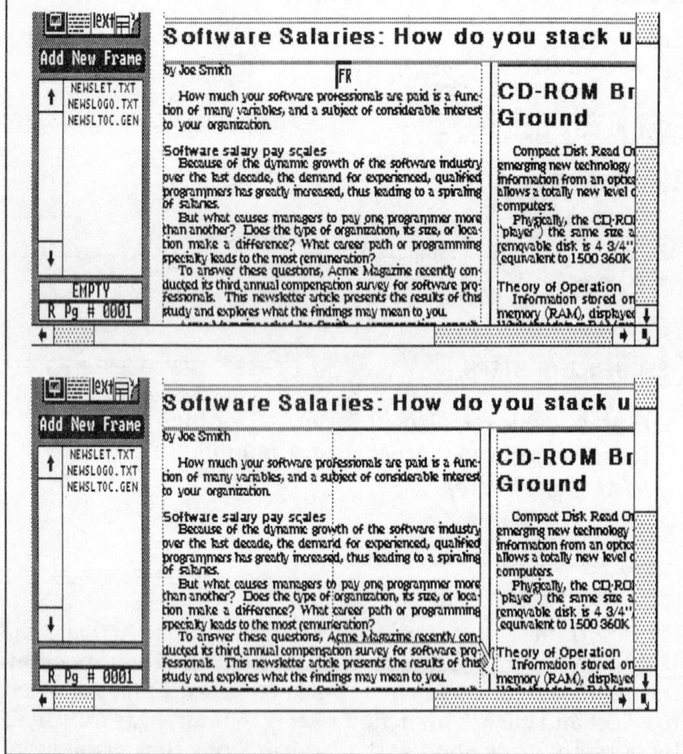

Figure 8: Creating a new frame

Selecting Multiple Frames To select multiple frames, hold down the Shift key as you click each one in succession. The word *Multiple* appears in the Current box. You can then move, resize, or cut/copy/paste these frames as a unit. To deselect one of the multiple frames, Shift-click the frame you want to deselect. You cannot select multiple frames to change their attributes (such as margins, columns, or frame background) or to assign the same Text/Picture file to frames simultaneously.

Selecting Frames beneath Frames To select a frame that is beneath another frame, use the Ctrl key as you click. With a pile of frames, each Ctrl-click selects the next frame in succession.

UNDO

To deselect one or all frames, select another frame or switch out of the Frame mode.

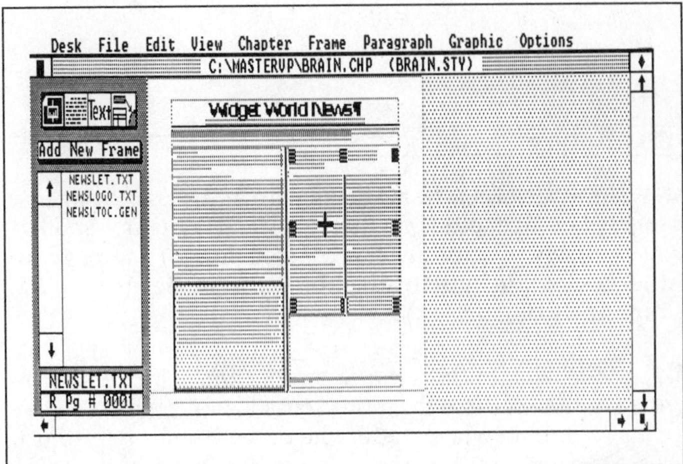

Figure 9: Frame selection handles

SEE ALSO

Cut/Copy/Paste; Mouse

Repositioning a Frame on the Same Page

SEQUENCE OF STEPS

Frame mode or (2.0 only) **Graphics** mode
[position the mouse within the frame]
[drag the frame to a new location]

or

Frame mode or (2.0 only) **Graphics** mode
[select the frame]
Frame menu
Sizing & Scaling
[adjust X and Y values]
OK or ↵

USAGE

You can reposition a frame elsewhere on the same page by using either the mouse or a dialog box; the latter method lets you precisely specify the frame's position on the page. In either case, begin by activating the Frame mode (or, with 2.0, Graphics mode).

Using the Mouse to Reposition a Frame To reposition with the mouse, place the mouse cursor, which will look like a plus sign, somewhere within the frame you wish to adjust. Press the mouse button and hold it while you drag to a new location. The mouse cursor changes to four arrowheads, and a ghosting frame moves with it. Release the mouse button and the frame snaps to its new location. (If you have difficulty placing the frame exactly where you want because it seems determined to land only in certain spots, see "Aligning Frames with Snap.") When you are repositioning a frame with the mouse, Ventura will not allow you to place the frame outside the edges of the page.

Providing Values to Reposition a Frame To position a frame according to values you provide, select the frame and use the Frame menu to display the Sizing & Scaling dialog box. To adjust the distance of the left edge of the frame from the left edge of the page, adjust the Upper Left X value. To change the distance of the top edge of the frame from the top edge of the page, change the Upper Left Y value. Give the OK and the frame will pop to its new location.

When repositioning with this dialog box, it is possible to place a frame outside the edges of the page. If this should happen, immediately invoke the dialog box again, while the frame is still selected. Provide more reasonable values to position the frame back on the page. Otherwise, you could find it difficult if not impossible to retrieve the frame since frames off the page cannot be selected with the mouse.

TIP

You can reposition and resize a frame (described below) at the same time. Use the Frame menu's Sizing & Scaling dialog box to provide values for X, Y, Height, and Width simultaneously (see Figure 10).

UNDO

You can change the frame back to its old location by following the same steps for repositioning.

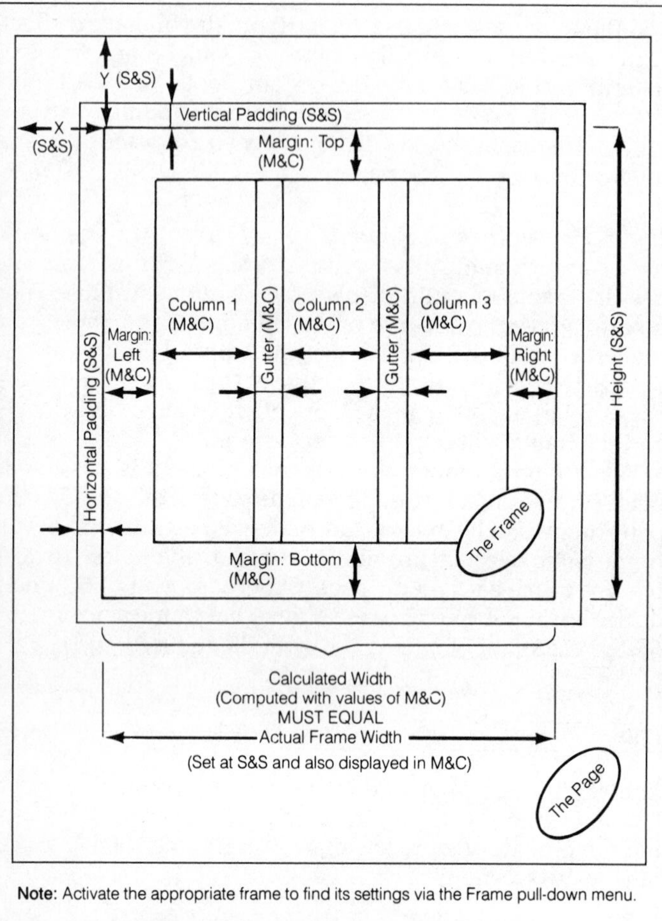

Note: Activate the appropriate frame to find its settings via the Frame pull-down menu.

M&C = Margins & Columns dialog box

S&S = Sizing & Scaling dialog box

If the frame is the same size as the page (i.e., you are working with the underlying-page frame), X and Y will be equal to 0, and Height and Width will match the page size.

Figure 10: Interaction of frame values

EXAMPLE

See Figure 11.

SEE ALSO

Mouse

Aligning Frames with Snap

SEQUENCE OF STEPS

Options menu
Turn Column Snap On/Turn Line Snap On

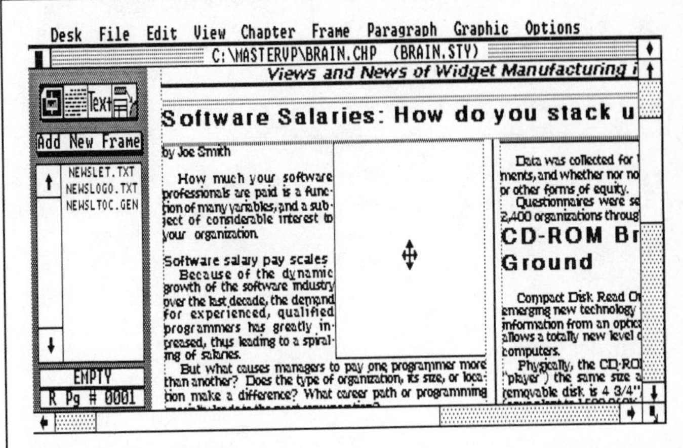

Figure 11: Repositioning a frame

USAGE

Using Column Snap causes standard frames to line up with columns that you've set for the underlying-page frame (using the Frame menu's Margins & Columns dialog box). To activate this feature, use the Options menu and choose **Turn Column Snap On**. Then, as you move the left or right edge of a standard frame with the mouse, the frame edge will snap to the column edges when it approaches them. (You can display the edges of the columns as light dashes by using the Options menu and choosing **Show Column Guides**.) This feature only affects frames as you create them or adjust the placement of their edges. It does not affect frames that are in place.

Using Line Snap makes the top and bottom edges of a frame line up with lines of Body Text that appear (or would appear) in the underlying-page frame. It uses the frame settings for the underlying-page frame and paragraph settings for the Body Text tag. The edges snap to the top edge of a line of the text. As with Column Snap, this feature affects frames only as you create or adjust them.

UNDO

To deactivate the Snap features, use the Options menu and choose either **Turn Column Snap Off** or **Turn Line Snap Off**.

SEE ALSO

Columns; Tags

Resizing Frames

SEQUENCE OF STEPS

Frame mode or (2.0 only) **Graphics** mode
[select frame]
[drag frame's handle]

or

Frame mode or (2.0 only) **Graphics** mode
[select frame]
Sizing & Scaling
[adjust **Frame Height** *and* **Frame Width***]*
OK or ↵

USAGE

You can use the mouse to change the size of frames, or you can use the Frame menu's Sizing & Scaling dialog box.

Using the Mouse to Resize Frames To change the size of a frame with the mouse, use the Frame mode (or Graphics mode in 2.0) to select the frame that you want to adjust. Then grab the frame by one of the handles and drag the handle to a new location. As you do, the mouse changes to a pointing finger, and a ghost of the frame will stretch or shrink along with the handle. Release the mouse button at the desired location and the frame will snap to the new size.

You may be able to combine the second two steps and select the frame at the same time you grab one of the handles. However, selecting the frame first makes the handles visible and allows you to grab one more easily.

If you have Line Snap or Column Snap turned on, as described above, the frame will snap into position as explained.

Providing Values to Resize Frames Instead of using the mouse, you can provide measurements to specify precise values for the size of the frame. In the Frame mode, select the frame you want to work with. Then use the Frame menu and choose **Sizing & Scaling**. In the resulting dialog box, you'll see the current dimensions of the box in the Frame Width and Frame Height fields. These values may have been set with the mouse. Adjust these values to adjust the size of the box.

For the underlying-page frame, these values will match those of the page, as specified by the Chapter menu's Page Layout dialog box. However, you can decrease these values to print a smaller area of the page, a useful way to print on pages smaller than standard sizes (see **Page Layouts**).

UNDO

Repeat the procedure with either the mouse or the dialog box to provide the original settings for the frame. If, when resizing with the mouse, you moved either the top or left edge of the frame and you want to undo with the dialog box, you may need to provide a different X (left offset) or Y (top offset) value (see "Repositioning a Frame on the Same Page," above).

SEE ALSO

Mouse

Running Text around Frames and Pictures

SEQUENCE OF STEPS

Frame mode or (2.0 only) **Graphics** mode
[create the frame if necessary]
[select the frame]

Frame menu
Sizing & Scaling
Flow Text Around: **On/Off**
OK or ↵

USAGE

The Flow Text Around setting determines whether text from the underlying-page frame remains outside a frame placed in front (on top) of it. The frame in front usually contains a picture, but can contain text, such as a callout, instead.

When you create a new (standard) frame, the Frame menu's Sizing & Scaling dialog box normally has Flow Text Around set to On for the new frame. This forces text that appears in the underlying-page frame to remain outside of the new frame.

If you set Text Flow Around: **Off**, the underlying text will flow behind the new frame, just as it would if the new frame weren't there. A graphic placed within the new frame will be superimposed on the underlying text.

The same happens when you begin with a standard frame that holds text and place another standard frame on top of it. The frame that you want to keep the text out of must be on top of the frame that contains the text. If this is not the case, you can place the flow-around frame on top by selecting it (with Ctrl-click), cutting it (with the Delete key), and pasting it on top (with the Insert key).

To create a text run-around—that is, text that follows the contours of an irregularly shaped picture—first create a frame that holds the picture. Select that frame and use the Frame menu's Sizing & Scaling dialog box to set Flow Text Around to **Off**. Text will flow beneath the frame, and the picture will appear superimposed on the text. Then, within the frame, create separate small frames that cover those areas of the picture that should be free of text (see Figure 14, below). The smaller frames (with Flow Text Around: **On**) will displace text from those areas and the text will flow around them.

When flowing text around a picture frame, it's generally best to place the frame all the way to one side or the other, as in Figure 12. This placement allows the reader to read the text easily. If you place the frame within the middle (left to right) of a column that holds text, text in the column will first flow down to the left side of the picture frame and then down to the right side, making the text hard to follow.

However, by using small frames you can still make the text flow from left to right, line by line, interrupted on each line by the picture. Before you create the picture frame, create a series of small frames, each one line high, that covers the area where the picture frame will be. Then place the big frame on top of these small frames and load the picture into it. (Note that unlike small frames used to create a text run-around, these frames must be no bigger than one line of text each.)

UNDO

With the frame selected, use the Frame menu's Sizing & Scaling dialog box. Switch the Flow Text Around setting to counteract the frame's effect you wish to change. To remove a series of unwanted small frames, Shift-click each one to select them as a multiple-frame grouping, then press the Delete key to cut them.

EXAMPLE

Figures 12 and 13 illustrate the difference between the On and Off settings for Flow Text Around; Figure 14 shows a text run-around.

SEE ALSO

Cut/Copy/Paste; Text; Text/Picture Files

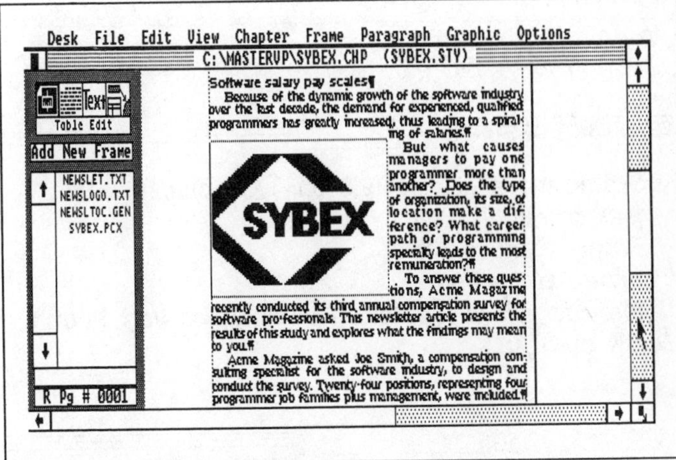

Figure 12: Flow Text Around: On

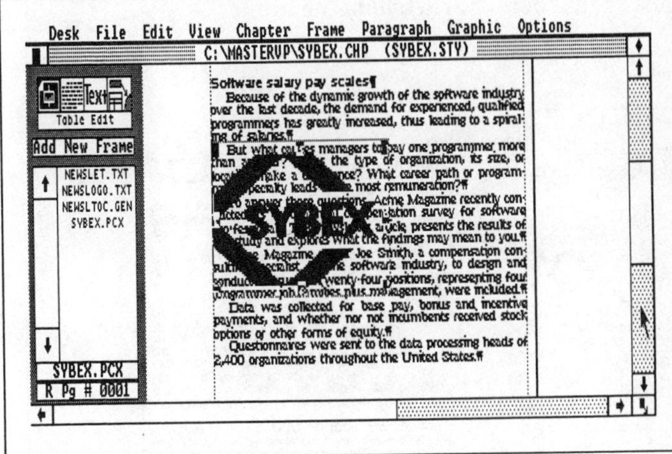

Figure 13: Flow Text Around: Off

Padding Frames

SEQUENCE OF STEPS

Frame mode or also (2.0 only) **Graphics** mode
[select frame]
Frame menu
Sizing & Scaling
[provide values for **Horiz Padding** *and* **Vert Padding***]*
OK or ↵

USAGE

Use padding to provide an area free of text around a frame. Note that padding controls the area *outside* the frame, while margins (set with the Frame menu/Margins & Columns) restrict the border area *within* the frame.

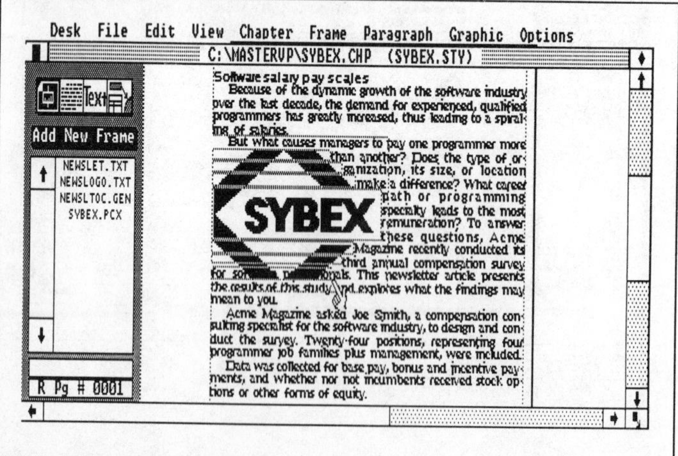

Figure 14: Text run-around

To provide padding for a frame, activate the Frame mode (or also , with 2.0, the Graphics mode) and select the frame. Use the Frame menu and choose **Sizing & Scaling**. To pad the left and right edges of the frame, provide a value for Horiz Padding. To pad the top and bottom edges, provide a value for Vert Padding. Then give the OK.

UNDO

With the frame selected, invoke the Frame menu's Sizing & Scaling dialog box. Move the keyboard cursor to the Horiz Padding and Vert Padding fields and remove the padding by deleting their values. You can use the Esc key to remove the numbers, which is the same as entering zero.

EXAMPLE

See Figure 15.

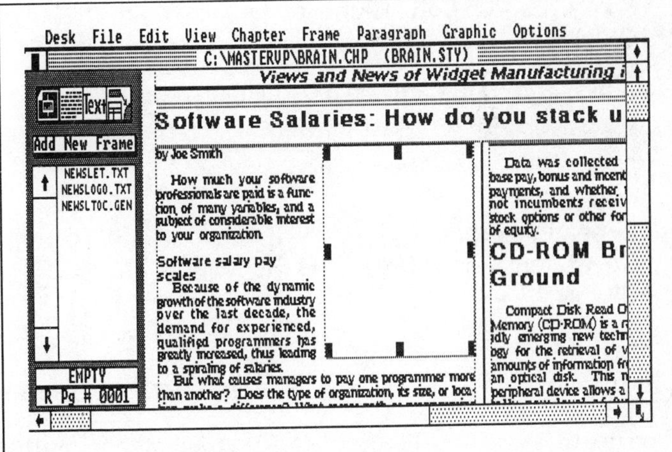

Figure 15: Frame padding

SEE ALSO

Margins

Repeating Frames

VERSION

2.0, 1.1, 1.0

SEQUENCE OF STEPS

To create a repeating frame:

> **Frame** mode
> *[create a standard frame]*
> *[optionally add text, picture, graphics]*
> *[optionally adjust the frame's attributes as desired]*
> **Frame** menu
> **Repeating Frame**
> For all Pages: **Left**, **Right**, or **Left & Right**
> **OK** or ↵

To hide a repeating frame on a particular page:

> **Frame** mode
> *[select the repeating frame]*
> **Frame** menu
> **Repeating Frame**
> On Current Page: **Hide This Repeating Frame**
> **OK** or ↵

USAGE

You use the Repeating Frame dialog box to create a frame that appears on every page (or on every left page or every right page) of the document. You can have up to six repeating frames to a chapter. You also use this dialog box to keep a repeating frame from showing on a particular page.

Creating a Repeating Frame In the Frame mode, begin by creating a standard frame (described above) on any page. If you're working with a double-sided document, as specified with the Page menu's Page Layout dialog box, create the frame on the same-sided page (left or right) that you want the repeating frame to appear on, unless you want it to appear on both sides, in which case it doesn't matter. Then, with the frame selected, assign the text file or picture file (see **Text/Picture Files**). You can also tie Ventura graphics to the frame using the Graphics mode. Set or adjust the frame's attributes, such as its placement on the page, margins, ruling lines and boxes. (You can make additional adjustments to the frame's attributes after you convert it to a repeating frame, at which time you can also assign or reassign a text/picture file.)

Then change the standard frame to a repeating frame as follows. Still in the Frame mode with the frame selected, pull down the Frame menu and select **Repeating Frame**. In the resulting dialog box, For All Pages will be set to **Off**. Change this setting to **Left**, **Right**, or **Left & Right**, depending on which pages of the document you want the repeating frame to appear on.

Using **Left & Right** will cause Ventura to create a mirror image of the repeating frame on pages opposite the one on which you create it; left and right margin values will be reversed, columns will remain the same. If desired, you can keep the margins from reflecting by creating the standard frame on a page and setting its attributes, and then copying the frame (with Shift-Del, for instance) to the facing page. Then separately convert these two frames appropriately to one-sided repeating frames.

With double-sided pages, using either **Left** or **Right** will cause the repeating frame to appear only on those respective pages. When using single-sided pages, use either the **Left & Right** button or the button (Left or Right) that agrees with the setting in the Current box.

Give the OK to create the repeating frame. If it is too long to fit entirely within a frame, a text file assigned to a repeating frame will continue from one page to the next, picking up where the file left off on the previous page. Frame Text—that is, text you type directly into the frame—will repeat from page to page, as headers and footers do. In fact, the two features can be combined (see **Headers and Footers**). When the same text file is also assigned to the underlying-page frame, on each page the text fills the underlying-page frame and, in the repeating frame, picks up where it left off.

Hiding a Repeating Frame on a Page To keep a repeating frame from showing on a particular page, go to the page on which you want to suppress the frame. Select the frame and use the Frame menu's Repeating Frame dialog box. Select **Hide This Repeating Frame**. When you give the OK, you'll still see the frame on the page; it will disappear when you select some other frame or change modes.

UNDO

To change a repeating frame back into a standard frame, go to the page on which you want the standard frame to appear. Select the repeating frame and, using the Frame menu's Repeating Frame dialog box, choose For All Pages: **Off**.

To remove a repeating frame completely, go to any page and change it into a standard frame. Then, with the standard frame selected, press the Delete key to cut the frame.

You can redisplay a repeating frame that's hidden on a particular page. If the frame is still showing and selected, use the Frame menu's Repeating Frame dialog box. Choose **Show This Repeating Frame** and give the OK. If the frame you want to display is not showing, click any frame (including the underlying-page frame) and, in the same dialog box, select **Show All Hidden Frames**. If you've hidden more than one frame on the page, they'll all reappear; you can then hide any that you don't want to show.

EXAMPLE

See Figure 16.

SEE ALSO

Cut/Copy/Paste; Page Format

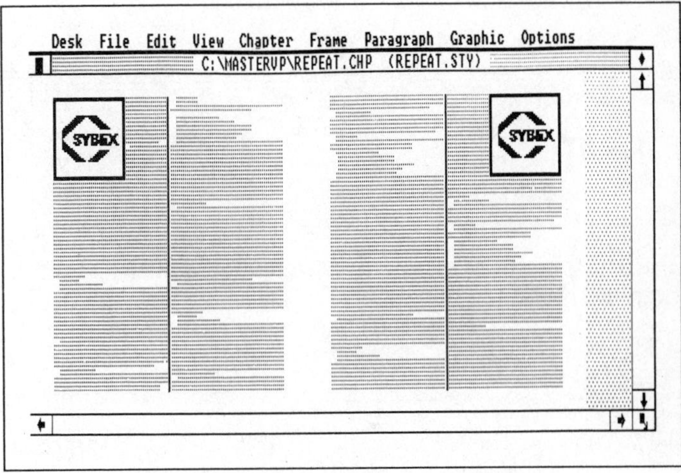

Figure 16: A repeating frame reflected on facing pages

Generated Elements

Generated files, see **Text/Picture Files**.
Generated frames, see **Frames**.
Generated tags, see **Tags**.

Graphics

Use the Graphics mode to draw with Ventura's built-in graphic shapes.

VERSION

2.0, 1.1, 1.0

USAGE

Any graphics you create will be tied to a frame (the host frame). Therefore, before drawing you should select the frame to which you want to tie the graphics.

When you reposition the frame on the same page or cut/copy/paste it elsewhere, the graphics adjust to the frame's new location automatically, staying in the same relative position. You can locate your graphics anywhere on the same page as the host frame, as close or as far away as you wish. The host frame need not contain anything (text or pictures).

If you neglect to select a host frame, Ventura will usually select the underlying-page frame as the host frame automatically. (Note that before version 2.0, graphics tied to the underlying-page frame automatically appear on every page sharing the same underlying-page frame. With 2.0, a graphic initially appears only on the page where you create it; more on this below).

Activating Graphics Mode

SEQUENCE OF STEPS

Graphics button or **View** menu/**Graphic Drawing** or **Ctrl-P**

USAGE

Use the Graphics mode to create or manipulate Ventura's built-in graphics. You can use any of three methods to activate the Graphics mode: click the **Graphics** button, which is the last of four buttons at the top of the Side-bar; pull down the View menu and click **Graphic Drawing**; or press **Ctrl-P** on the keyboard.

UNDO

Use one of the methods for switching Ventura to one of its other modes (Frame, Paragraph, or Text mode).

EXAMPLE

See Figure 17.

SEE ALSO

Frames; Side-bar; Tags; Text

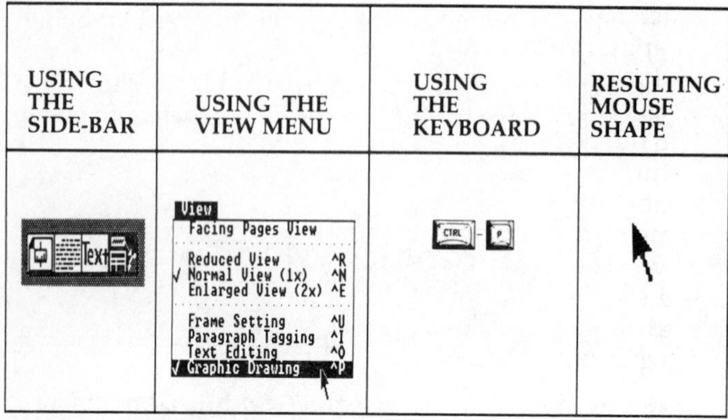

Figure 17: Activating Graphics mode

Graphics Grid

SEQUENCE OF STEPS

Graphics mode
Graphic menu
Grid Settings
[provide value for **Horizontal Spacing** *and* **Vertical Spacing***]*
OK or ↵

USAGE

The graphics grid is an invisible set of predetermined points to which graphics will "snap" (align automatically) as you work with them. The grid works in a manner similar to that of Column Snap and Line Snap for standard frames. Before creating a Ventura graphic, decide if you want to use the graphic grid and, if so, in what increments.

Switch to the Graphics mode and select **Grid Settings** on the Graphic menu. In the resulting dialog box, set Grid Snap to **On**. Provide values for Horizontal Spacing and for Vertical Spacing. Give the OK. Then draw your graphic. Its edges will snap to the invisible grid that you established.

Ventura graphics, unlike frames, do not have a dialog box for establishing width and height. The only way to establish the dimensions of a graphic precisely is to use a graphics grid when you create or resize a graphic.

Grid settings are specific to the frame that your graphics are tied to. If you switch frames, you'll find that you can switch grid settings as well.

Drawing Graphics

SEQUENCE OF STEPS

Graphics mode
[select host frame (use Frame mode before 2.0)]
[click desired icon]
[position mouse at desired top-left corner]
[drag to desired bottom-right corner and release]

To draw multiple graphics of the same type:

Shift-drag

To draw perfect circles, squares, and angled lines:

Alt-drag

USAGE

To draw a graphic, first select a frame to which you want to tie the graphic. (Before version 2.0, you must use the Frame mode to do this; with 2.0 you can use the Graphics mode.)

Click one of the five drawing icons on the Side-bar that represents the graphic shape you desire; when you move the mouse cursor, it changes into the icon's corresponding shape (see Figure 18).

Place the mouse in the top-left corner of the position you want for your graphic. Press and hold the mouse button and, as you hold, drag the mouse to the bottom-right corner you desire and release. The graphic will appear.

TIP

You can keep the same icon active by holding down the Shift key as you draw. In addition, with release 2.0, you can restrict your drawings to squares (no rectangles), circles (no ellipses), and lines of 45 degree increments by holding down the Alt key as you draw.

SEE ALSO

Frames

Selecting and Manipulating Graphics

SEQUENCE OF STEPS

To select a graphic

Frame mode (1.1 and 1.0 only)
[click host frame] (1.1 and 1.0 only)
Graphics mode
[click Selection icon if necessary]
[click graphic in working area]

GRAPHIC NAME	SIDE-BAR MENU	MOUSE CURSOR SHAPE
Box Text	 BOX TEXT	
Line		
Circle		
Rectangle		
Rounded Rectangle		

Figure 18: Graphic drawing icons and corresponding mouse cursor shapes

To select a graphic beneath another graphic

Ctrl-click

To select multiple graphics

Shift-click

To select all graphics

Graphics menu
Select All

or

Ctrl-Q

USAGE

Use these procedures to select a graphic so that you can change its attributes, move it, change its size, or cut or copy it.

In the Graphics mode, the Selection icon (which looks like an arrow) on the Side-bar should be darkened, unless you've been creating multiple graphics. If not, click it with the mouse. Then use the mouse to click the graphic you want to work with in the working area. Once selected, the graphic acquires up to eight black handles. Ghosting selection handles will appear on the host frame.

A newly created graphic is selected automatically, as is a newly pasted graphic (see **Cut/Copy/Paste**).

You can stretch or shrink the graphic by dragging the selection handles; the mouse cursor looks like a pointing hand. You can move the graphic elsewhere on the same page by dragging a selected graphic from within the graphic; the mouse cursor looks like four arrowheads.

Selecting Multiple Graphics To select multiple graphics, hold down the Shift key as you click each with the mouse. To deselect one of multiple graphics, Shift-click it again. You can stretch, shrink, reposition or cut/copy multiple graphics as a unit. You can also change their line and fill attributes (described below) at one time as well. (You cannot change the attributes of multiply selected frames or paragraph tags.)

Selecting Graphics Beneath Graphics To select a graphic that's below one or more other graphics, hold the Ctrl key as you click the graphic. In a pile of graphics, Ventura initially selects the graphic on top. Each Ctrl-click selects the next graphic in succession, to start again with the top graphic after the one on the bottom.

Selecting All Graphics To select all the graphics associated with a frame, first use the Frame mode (or also, with 2.0, Graphics mode) to select the host frame. Then, in Graphics mode (or also, with 2.0, Frame mode), pull down the Graphic menu and choose **Select All**. Alternatively, use **Ctrl-Q**.

With multiple frames and multiple graphics, you can see quickly which graphics are associated with a given frame. Once you find the frame you are looking for, its graphics are selected so you can easily work with them as a unit, if desired.

UNDO

To deselect one or more graphics, click an area outside the graphic or select another graphic or change modes. To deselect one of multiple graphics, Shift-click the graphic. To select another graphic in a pile, Ctrl-click successively.

EXAMPLE

See Figure 19.

SEE ALSO

Cut/Copy/Paste; Frames

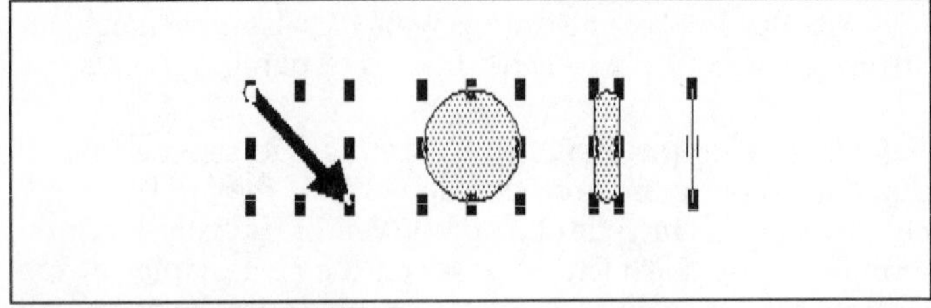

Figure 19: Selected graphics

Graphics Line Attributes

SEQUENCE OF STEPS

(1.1, 1.0) **Frame** mode/*[select host frame]*
Graphics mode
[select graphic]
Ctrl-L or **Graphic** menu/**Line Attributes**
[select attributes]
OK or ↵

Use this procedure to assign attributes (thickness, color, arrowheads, and so on) to lines created with Ventura graphics, including arrows, circles, rectangles, rounded rectangles, and box text. For filled-in graphics, such as a solid circle or rectangle, the line attributes you assign regulate the outline of the graphic.

In the Graphics mode, select the graphic by clicking it in the working area. (You can Shift-click to select multiple graphics to adjust.) Then pull down the Graphic menu and choose **Line Attributes** (or type **Ctrl-L**).

In the Line Attributes dialog box, you can adjust the thickness of the line by using one of the Thickness settings. There are five standard thickness setting, but you can select **Custom**

Width and provide your own value. The standard thickness settings are as follows:

SETTING	FRACTIONAL POINTS	INCHES
Thin	0.06	0.001
2	1.26	0.018
3	3.66	0.051
4	9.00	0.125
Thick	18.00	0.25

Initially Ventura provides a line with a custom thickness of .24 fractional points (.003 inches), which places its thickness between the Thin and 2 settings.

You can also use this dialog box to adjust the color of the line (see **Color**). The actual effects you see may be restricted by your monitor and printer. By specifying White, you cause the line to seem to disappear. However, as long as you don't set Thickness to none, the line is still there, and you would be able to see it if the graphic should partially hide some text or other graphic.

Use the **End Styles** grouping to indicate the manner in which the line terminates. You can end the line squared off, rounded, or with an arrowhead. Ventura places a check mark next to your choice. The left column of symbols regulates whichever end of the line you created first; the right column regulates the other end. The End Styles settings apply only to lines created with the line icon. They have no effect on the outline of other graphic shapes.

Use the **Save To** button to set aside a copy of this dialog box's settings for use with a similar type of graphic you plan to create. For existing graphics, you can make the settings replicate the saved settings by clicking the **Load From** button.

UNDO

With the graphic selected, use the Graphic menu's Line Attributes dialog box or Ctrl-L. Set Thickness to **None** to remove all line attributes from a given graphic.

SEE ALSO

Color; Line Drawing

Graphics Fill Attributes

SEQUENCE OF STEPS

(1.1, 1.0) **Frame** mode/*[select host frame]*
Graphics mode
[select graphic]
Ctrl-F or **Graphic menu/Fill Attributes**
[select attributes]
OK or ↵

USAGE

Use the Fill Attributes dialog box to adjust any pattern and color that will fill the circles, rectangles, rounded rectangles, and box text. You cannot use this procedure with lines (including arrows).

In the Graphics mode, select the graphic by clicking it in the working area. (You can shift-click to select multiple graphics to adjust.) Then pull down the Graphic menu and choose **Fill Attributes** (or type **Ctrl-F**).

As described with Line Attributes above, use the Fill Attributes dialog box to specify Color and Pattern. Figure 20 shows the seven standard patterns that Ventura uses to fill graphics and for box text, frame backgrounds, and ruling lines and boxes. Initially, graphics use pattern 4 in Black.

Choose **Transparent** if you want text and other graphics that are placed underneath the graphic to show through. To obtain this effect, Pattern must not be set to Solid. By selecting **Opaque**, you hide material beneath the selected graphic. For Opaque to work, Pattern must not be set to Hollow (see Figure 21). The capacity to hide material also depends upon the abilities of your printer.

To transfer the settings from one similar graphic to another, use the Load From and Save To buttons in the same manner described for Line Attributes above.

After adjusting the fill attributes, you may find that they don't take effect and the graphic looks just as it did. If so, "re-ink" the screen by pressing the Esc key.

UNDO

With the graphic selected, use the Graphic menu's Fill Attributes dialog box or Ctrl-F. Set Pattern to Hollow to remove all fill attributes from a given graphic.

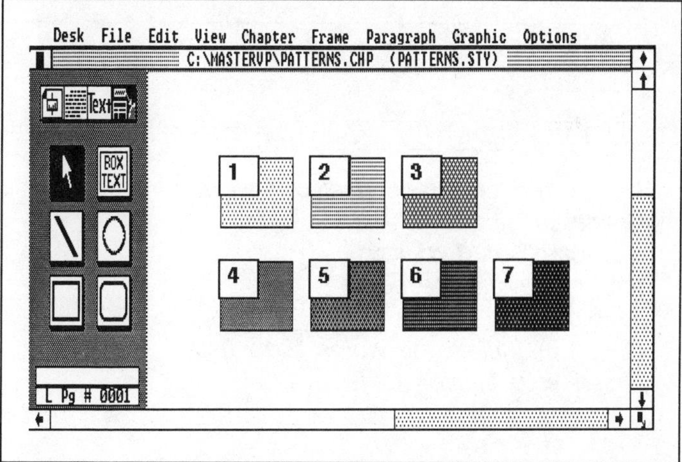

Figure 20: Ventura's seven fill patterns

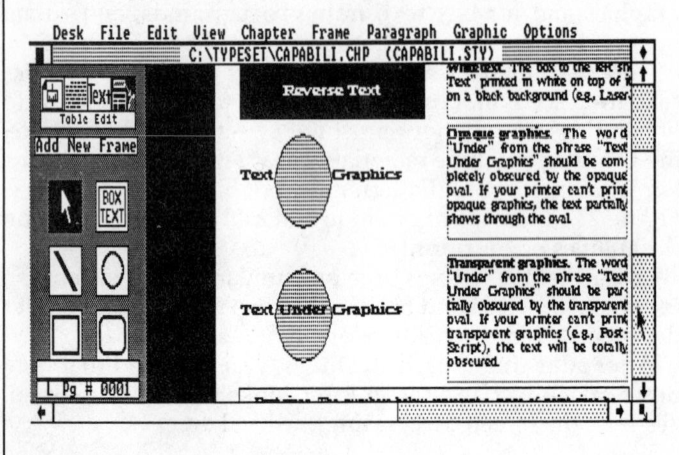

Figure 21: Opaque and transparent graphics

SEE ALSO

Color; Frames

Box Text

SEQUENCE OF STEPS

(1.1, 1.0) **Frame** mode/*[select host frame]*
Graphics mode
Side-bar: **Box Text** icon
[drag to create the box]
Text mode
(1.1, 1.0) *[delete the words "Box Text"]*
[insert your desired text]

USAGE

Use the Box Text feature to create a text-holding box that's tied to a frame. You can provide a Box Text box with attributes just as you can other graphics, or you can eliminate the attributes so that only the text shows. (With versions 1.1 and 1.0, box text tied to the underlying-page frame appears on each page.)

To create a Box Text box, select the host frame. Then choose the **Box Text** icon. Move the mouse to the working area and the mouse cursor changes to the letters *Te*, cornered within a bracket. Place the mouse in the top-left position you want for the Box Text and drag to the bottom-right (the mouse cursor looks like a pointing hand). Release and the box appears along with the square-shaped end mark (□). To insert your text within the box, switch to the Text mode. Place the text cursor in front of the end mark and then type in your text. (In versions 1.1 and 1.0, the words *Box Text* also appear in front of the end mark. Delete these words and then type in your text.)

You cannot assign box text to a standard word-processed file (or vice versa) as you can with frames. Ventura stores the text for Box Text in the chapter's CAP file. This file has the same name (and directory location) as the chapter file, but with a CAP extension. You can use your word processor to run the spelling checker or otherwise edit this file in ASCII mode, but do not remove or insert returns. (Ventura also stores captions and Frame Text in this file.)

You can assign attributes to the box by selecting the box as you would any graphic and using the Graphics menu. Providing the box with a Black Solid fill attribute automatically changes the text font to white.

You can format the Box Text tag by using paragraph mode and clicking some box text. The name of the box text tag, Z_BOXTEXT, will appear in the Current box toward the bottom of the Side-bar. Use the Paragraph menu to change its attributes (see **Tags**).

UNDO

To remove a Box Text box, use Graphics mode to select the box. Cut it by using the Delete key.

EXAMPLE

See Figure 22.

SEE ALSO

Cut/Copy/Paste; Tags; Text

Rearranging Piled Graphics

SEQUENCE OF STEPS

(1.1, 1.0) **Frame** mode/*[select host frame]*
Graphics mode
[select graphic]
Graphic/**Send To Back** (Ctrl-Z) or Graphic/**Bring To Front** (Ctrl-A)

USAGE

Use these commands on the Graphic menu or their Ctrl key shortcuts to rearrange the placement of a graphic in a pile of graphics. Ventura places newly created or pasted graphics in front (on top) of other graphics. (You can also use cutting and pasting to rearrange graphics; see **Cut/Copy/Paste**.)

In Graphics mode, select the graphic. If it is completely beneath (behind) others in a pile, you will need to use Ctrl-click, as described above, to select the graphic. To send the graphic to the back of the pile (furthest from you as you view the screen), press **Ctrl-Z** or, using the Graphic menu, choose

Send To Back. To bring the graphic to the top of the pile, press **Ctrl-A** or use the Graphic menu and choose **Bring To Front**.

UNDO

To undo the effects of one of these procedures, use the procedures to rearrange other graphics in the pile.

SEE ALSO

Cut/Copy/Paste

Repeating Graphics

VERSION

2.0 only

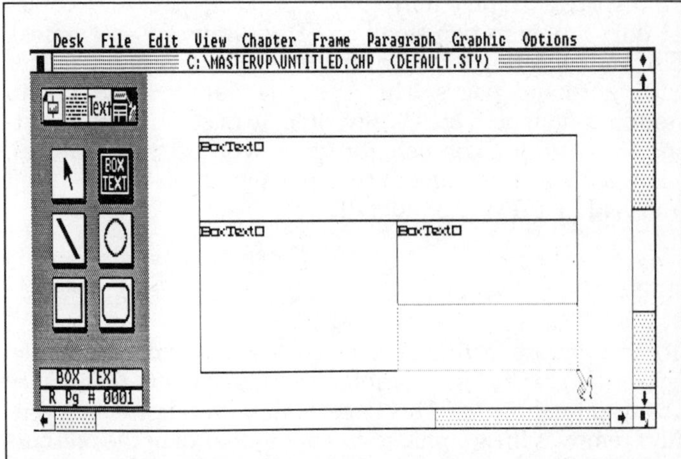

Figure 22: Box text

SEQUENCE OF STEPS

Graphics mode
[select the graphic]
Graphic menu
Show On All Pages

USAGE

With release 2.0, graphics tied to the underlying-page frame no longer automatically repeat on every page of the document. This procedure allows you to have a graphic do that, without having to tie it to a repeating frame.

Activate the Graphics mode and select the graphic. Use the Graphic menu and choose **Show On All Pages**. The graphic will then appear in the same location in all pages of the document, even when you're using double-sided pages (specified with Chapter menu/Page Size & Layout).

TIP

To display a graphic mirrored on opposite pages, tie copies of the graphic to two small repeating frames (see **Frames**). Use one repeating frame for the left-hand pages and one for the right-hand pages. The repeating frames need contain nothing and would thus be invisible. To make sure the repeating frames don't compete for space with existing material, place them in a margin or use Frame menu/Sizing & Scaling and set Flow Text Around: **Off**.

UNDO

To change a repeating graphic back to a standard graphic, select the graphic. The Graphic menu's Show On All Pages changes to Show On This Page. Check this choice and Ventura removes the graphic from pages other than the one currently displayed.

Headers/Footers

Use headers and footers, respectively, to create text that appears at the top and bottom of each page in the document.

VERSION

2.0, 1.1, 1.0

USAGE

Ventura allows you to have headers and footers of one or two lines each. (You can augment with Frame Text in a repeating frame if you need more lines, see **Frames**.) Headers and footers can appear flush left, centered, or flush right on the page. In addition, with double-sided pages you can have separate sets of headers and footers for left- and right-hand pages. You can also place separate headers in any of the three positions on the same page, though there is some risk of overlapping.

Creating Headers and Footers

SEQUENCE OF STEPS

(2.0) **Chapter** menu or (1.1 and 1.0) **Page** menu
Headers & Footers
[for each Define button, provide specifications]
OK or ↵

USAGE

Use the Chapter menu's (Page menu before version 2.0) Headers & Footers dialog box to trigger Ventura's header/footer system and to specify the text that appears at the top and bottom of each page. In the Define grouping of the dialog box are four buttons:

Left Page Header	Right Page Header
Left Page Footer	Right Page Footer

Each button has independent settings for the remaining categories in the dialog box. By clicking a button, you display the settings that apply to it. When no headers or footers show, for each Define button Usage is set to Off. To use a header or footer, first click the Define button that corresponds to the position you desire. You can use only sides for which your document is set up (see **Page Formats**). Then click the **On** button.

Next fill in the Left/Center/Right fields as applicable. This determines the text's horizontal placement on the page for the Define location you chose. If you place too much text in adjacent fields, there may be overlapping.

Repeat the process by clicking other buttons in the Define grouping for which you want to provide text. Give the OK and the header(s) or footer(s) you've set will appear in the document, within a generated frame. You can adjust characteristics of the generated frame if you wish (see **Frames**).

Using Inserts As you fill in the Left/Center/Right fields, you can use the buttons in the Inserts grouping. Most of these buttons insert codes onto the field line that has the text cursor at the time that you click. Ventura will replace the code with appropriate information in the document. You can also enter a code simply by typing it in yourself.

Clicking the **Chapter #** button inserts the code [C#] on the line with the text cursor. Ventura will replace this code with the chapter number, as set by the Chapter menu's Update Counters dialog box. Clicking **Page #** inserts the code [P#], which Ventura replaces with the current page number. For more on these two codes, see **Numbering Adjustments**.

Clicking the **1st Match** button inserts the code *[<tag name]*; replace the words *tag name* with the name of an actual tag. Then, in place of the code, Ventura will display the text of the first paragraph on the page which matches the tag. If no paragraph with the specified tag appears on the page, Ventura uses the text of the previous occurrence. Likewise, clicking the **Last Match** button inserts the code *[>tag name]*. Replace *tag name* with the name of a tag and Ventura will use the text of the last paragraph so tagged on the page.

When you click the **Text Attr** button, Ventura inserts the code *<D>*. Replace the letter *D* with a text attribute code (see Appendix C) to turn effects on and off as you would with a text file and a word processor.

For double-sided documents, you can reflect your header or footer settings to those for the opposite page. After you set up the header or footer for one side, choose **Copy To Facing Page**.

UNDO

Using the Chapter menu's Headers & Footers dialog box, click the Define button for the position you want to turn off, and then click Usage: **Off**. Follow this procedure for each Usage position you want to undo. Text entered on the field lines will ghost and become available again should you set Usage: **On**.

To delete individual entries in the Left/Center/Right fields, position the text cursor in the desired field and press the Esc key.

EXAMPLE

For a left page header set up as

Left: Page [P#]
Center: The Brainstorm

and reflected to the right page by clicking Copy To Facing Page, the document would appear as shown in Figure 23 for

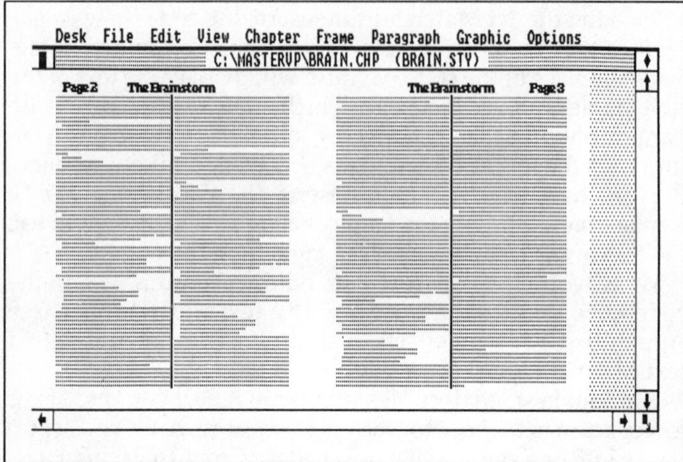

Figure 23: Double-sided header

pages 2 and 3 of a double-sided document that begins on the right page.

SEE ALSO

Frames; Tags; Text

Suppressing Headers and Footers Page by Page

SEQUENCE OF STEPS

[go to the appropriate page]
(2.0) **Chapter** menu or (1.1, 1.0) **Page** menu
Turn Header Off or **Turn Footer Off**

USAGE

Use this procedure to turn off the header or footer that appears on a particular page. Ventura will remove the header or footer along with its generated frame, freeing up the space for use by the underlying-page frame or another frame.

First, display the page from which you want to remove the header or footer. Then use the Chapter menu (Page menu before version 2.0) and choose **Turn Header Off** or **Turn Footer Off**, as appropriate. If the menu says Turn Header (Footer) On, the header or footer is already turned off for that page.

Do not use this procedure for page after page to turn off the header or footer in an entire document. To do that, use the Chapter or Page menu's Header & Footer dialog box, as described above.

UNDO

To allow the header or footer to reappear on a page for which you've suppressed it, go to the page, use the Chapter or Page menu, and choose **Turn Header On** or **Turn Footer On**. If it says Turn Header (Footer) Off, the header or footer for the page is already on.

Header and Footer Tags

SEQUENCE OF STEPS

Paragraph mode
[click text in the header or footer]
Paragraph menu
[use dialog box]
OK or ↵
[tag other paragraphs if desired]

USAGE

You can change the attributes of a header's or footer's generated tag and in so doing change the display of current or future text. In Paragraph mode, click the text appearing in the header or footer. For headers, the tag name *Z_HEADER* will appear in the Current box toward the bottom of the Sidebar. For footers, the tag name *Z_FOOTER* will appear. You can then use any of the dialog boxes that spring from the Paragraph menu to adjust paragraph attributes.

You won't see these tag names on the Paragraph mode's Assignment list unless you used the Options menu's Set Preferences dialog box to choose Generated Tags: **Shown.**

SEE ALSO

Tags

Hyphenation/Dashes

Ventura provides a variety of ways to hyphenate text.

VERSION

2.0, 1.1, 1.0 (Some features, such as second algorithm and successive hyphen control, are not available for 1.0.)

USAGE

You can set hyphenation by the paragraph tag. You can also enter several types of hyphens directly into text, either with

Ventura or with your word processor. Ventura also gives you control over its hyphenation dictionaries, and thus you can show Ventura how to hyphenate words by the tag.

Hyphenation with Paragraph Tags

SEQUENCE OF STEPS

Paragraph mode
[select a paragraph]
Paragraph menu
Alignment
Hyphenation: **USENGLSH** *[or other appropriate choice if available]*
OK *or* ↵

USAGE

Use this procedure to activate standard American English hyphenation of words in all paragraphs to which you've applied a certain tag. (To hyphenate according to another set of rules, see the following section.) In Paragraph mode, select a sample paragraph tagged as desired. Use the Paragraph menu and select **Alignment**. In the dialog box, for Hyphenation choose **USENGLSH**. (If more than one USENGLSH button appears, you can use either one.) Give the OK and Ventura will hyphenate all paragraphs with that tag. Ventura uses the algorithm (program procedure) contained in the file USENGLSH.HY1 to determine where and when words should be hyphenated.

Hyphenating with a Second Algorithm With versions 2.0 and 1.1, you can have Ventura hyphenate with one of its secondary algorithms. The file names for these algorithms are

SPANISH.HY2

FRENCH.HY2

GERMAN.HY2 (version 2.0 only)

ITALIAN.HY2

UKENGLSH.HY2

USENGLS2.HY2

Use one of these to provide hyphenation according to the rules of British English or another language or for more thorough (although slower) American English hyphenation (USENGLS2.HY2). Use one of these by copying one (and only one) from the Loadable Filter disk (#3) into the VENTURA directory. Once you do, the file name will appear in the Paragraph menu's Alignment dialog box as the second Hyphenation choice. You can then have Ventura use the secondary algorithm on tagged paragraphs by selecting that setting.

Restricting Repeated Hyphenation You can restrict the number of successive lines that Ventura hyphenates. In the Paragraph menu's Alignment dialog box, use the buttons for Successive Hyphens (1 to 5 or Unlimited). More than two lines hyphenated successively is generally considered undesirable, unless this restriction results in loose lines.

UNDO

To turn off the hyphenation associated with a tag, use the Paragraph mode. With a sample paragraph selected, use the Paragraph menu and select **Alignment**. Then choose Hyphenation: **Off**. Choose **USENGLSH** to go back to standard hyphenation.

SEE ALSO

Tags

Hyphenation with the Keyboard and Your Word Processor

SEQUENCE OF STEPS

To have Ventura identify loose lines for you in justified text (set with Paragraph menu/Alignment dialog box):

Options menu
Show Loose Lines

To insert a standard hyphen, discretionary hyphen, en dash or em dash:

[turn hyphenation for the tag on or off as appropriate]
[insert appropriate hyphen]

USAGE

Use hyphens to tighten loose text—that is, justified text with an inordinate amount of white space between words. To have Ventura flag loose lines for you, use the Options menu and select **Show Loose Lines**. Ventura will display the lines in reverse video.

You may also wish to use hyphens to reduce extreme raggedness (sometimes called "buck teeth") in left-aligned text. However, Ventura will not flag lines when they're not justified. Of course, you could temporarily justify the text, insert hyphens into loose lines, and then reset the alignment.

Use the keyboard to insert hyphens within or between words in the working area of Ventura. For hyphens to show at the end of a line, you must first turn the hyphenation for the tag on, as described earlier. None of the following hyphens/dashes will appear split at the end of the line if hyphenation for the tag is turned off. If hyphenation is off, these hyphens will keep all text on either side of them (until a blank space) on the same line.

TYPE OF HYPHEN/ DASH	IN VENTURA	IN WORD PROCESSOR
Standard hyphen	Hyphen key	Hyphen key
Discretionary hyphen	Ctrl-hyphen	<-> or word processor's method
En dash	Alt-196 (on keypad) or Ctrl-[	<196>
Em dash	Alt-197 (on keypad) or Ctrl-]	<197>or -- (two hyphens converted; see below)

A standard hyphen always appears, even within a line. Use a standard hyphen between words joined by a hyphen, such as compound modifiers. A discretionary hyphen appears in print only when the word you insert it in straddles a line break. On the screen, it will also appear within the line (as a chunky hyphen) if you have tabs and returns showing (use **Ctrl-T** or the Options menu's **Show Tabs & Returns**). When a discretionary hyphen is to the right of the keyboard cursor (in Text mode), the words *Discr. Hyphen 1* appear in the Current box. To keep a word from being hyphenated, place a discretionary hyphen at the beginning of the word.

With your word processor, you can create a discretionary hyphen by either entering **<->** or using the word processor's own means of creating discretionary hyphens (Microsoft Word and WordPerfect: Ctrl-hyphen; WordStar: Ctrl-OE).

Use an en dash between continuing numbers. Use an em dash to signal a sudden break in thought within a sentence or to introduce an explanation. En dashes and em dashes always appear and aren't generally available in word processors.

You can use two hyphens (--) in word processor text to indicate an em dash and have Ventura convert them automatically when it loads the text file. Use the Option menu's Set Preferences dialog box. Set Auto-Adjustments to " and **--**, which also converts inch marks (") to true quotes

(“ ”). Setting Auto Adjustment to **Both** adjusts hyphens, inch marks, and styles as well (see **Fonts**).

UNDO

Delete inappropriate hyphens, either with Ventura in Text mode or with your word processor.

EXAMPLES

Standard hyphen:

> A well-conceived idea of the mayor-elect.

Discretionary hyphen; appears when needed at the end of a line:

> key-
> board

but disappears when the word falls within the line:

> keyboard

En dash:

> During the week of August 22–26,
> turn in pages 30–40.

In the word processor, this appears as

> During the week of August 22<196>26, turn in pages 30<196>40.

Em dash:

> An em dash—a character sometimes simply called a dash, which you simulate on the typewriter with two hyphens—can be used to separate the main parts of a sentence, as in this example.

which, in the word processor, may appear as

> An Em dash<197>a character sometimes simply called a dash, which you simulate on the typewriter with two hyphens<197>can be used to separate the main parts of a sentence, as in this example.

SEE ALSO

Text

Hyphenation Dictionaries

SEQUENCE OF STEPS

[use your word processor to edit and save the HYPHUSER.DIC file as ASCII text]

USAGE

The HYPHUSER.DIC file contains words that Ventura consults in addition to the algorithm you specify (with the Paragraph menu's Alignment dialog box) and Ventura's exception dictionary (HYPHEXPT.DIC). Use HYPHUSER.DIC to indicate hyphenation for words that are not correctly hyphenated by the algorithm or the exception dictionary but that you expect Ventura to encounter repeatedly in your documents. Enter words one to a line, with a standard hyphen (use the hyphen key) indicating where you want Ventura to hyphenate when necessary. If you want Ventura to keep from hyphenating a word at all times, enter the word into the dictionary without a hyphen.

UNDO

Use your word processor in ASCII mode to remove words from the HYPHUSER.DIC file that you don't want treated in this special fashion.

EXAMPLE

Enter

key-board

to have Ventura hyphenate this word at a line break. Enter

Ventura

to keep Ventura from hyphenating its own name.

Indents and Outdents

This procedure indents or outdents the first line(s) of all paragraphs so tagged.

VERSION

2.0, 1.1, 1.0

SEQUENCE OF STEPS

Paragraph mode
[click a sample paragraph]
Paragraph menu
Alignment
First Line: **Indent** *or* **Outdent**
In/Outdent Width: *[provide a value]*
(2.0, 1.1) In/Outdent Height: *[provide a value]*
OK *or* ↵

USAGE

Figure 24 shows the effects you can achieve by indenting or outdenting the first line or lines of a paragraph.

In Paragraph mode, choose a paragraph whose tag you want to attribute this characteristic to. Then use the Paragraph menu and select **Alignment**. Set First line to **Indent** or **Outdent** as appropriate. Then provide a value for In/Outdent Width, the additional distance of the first line(s) with respect to the remainder of the paragraph. Then, if you want to affect more than one line, move to In/Outdent Height and enter the number of lines (default is 1). Give the OK.

In the same dialog box, you may notice a setting for Relative Indent. Leave the setting on Off except when you use it in conjunction with the Paragraph menu's Breaks dialog box to create multitag paragraphs (see **Breaking Paragraphs**).

When you provide an outdent to a paragraph, there must be enough blank space to the left of the paragraph to accommodate the protruding text. You can provide additional space by increasing the left margin of the frame that holds the text (see **Margins**). Or you can increase the distance the paragraph is set in from the left (see **Spacing**).

UNDO

With the paragraph selected, use the Paragraph menu and choose **Alignment**. Press the Esc key to delete the value for In/Outdent Width and give the OK.

EXAMPLE

See Figure 24.

SEE ALSO

Breaking Paragraphs; Margins; Spacing; Tags

Indexing

Ventura can compile and format an index for your document in several ways.

This paragraph has a first-line indent of 1/2 inch. Notice how the first line sinks into the main body of text. To achieve this effect, use the Paragraph menu's Alignment command. Set First Line to Indent. For In/Outdent Width, specify .5 inches.

This paragraph has the first three lines indented 1/2 inch. Notice how the first three lines sink into the main body of text. To achieve this effect, use the Paragraph menu's Alignment command. Set First Line to Indent. For In/Outdent Width, specify .5 inches. For In/Outdent Height, specify 3 lines.

This paragraph has a first-line outdent of 1/2 inch. Notice how the first line protrudes from the main body of text. To achieve this effect, use the Paragraph menu's Alignment command. Set First Line to Outdent. For In/Outdent Width, specify .5 inches.

Figure 24: First line indents and outdents

VERSION

2.0, 1.1, 1.0

USAGE

To create an index for a document, you must first insert index entries into your document to flag those locations you want Ventura to index. Each page that you want included in the index reference must have an index entry, but you can copy an index entry to additional pages. You can also have Ventura automatically generate a series of index entries on successive pages by using its header/footer feature. You can make index entries with your word processor, and you can use your word processor's capacity to copy them.

Once you have the index entries in place, you make Ventura compile the index, formatted as you indicate. The resulting generated file is like any other text file. You can load it into an otherwise empty chapter by using the File menu's Load Text/Picture command (Text Format: **Generated**) and then print the index chapter alone or as part of a publication.

Creating Entries in Text

SEQUENCE OF STEPS

Text mode
[position keyboard cursor]

(Version 2.0)	(Versions 1.1 and 1.0)
Ctrl-C or	**Edit** menu
Edit Menu/**Ins Special Item**	
F3 or **Index Entry**	**Insert/Edit Index**

(All versions)
[provide entry information]
OK or ↵

USAGE

In the Text mode, place the keyboard cursor in the spot you want Ventura to use in determining the page number. Then use Ctrl-C or the Edit menu and select **Ins Special Item.** Then click **Index**. Then press **F3** or click **Index Entry**. The resulting dialog box has three alternatives for Type Of Entry: Index, See, and See Also. Normally, you select **Index**. Use **See** to create a cross reference for a topic for which you don't provide other entries that generate page numbers. Use **See Also** for topics for which you both provide other entries that generate page numbers *and* need an entry to direct the reader elsewhere as well. (Once Ventura generates your index, be sure to proof it for proper use of See and See Also. Correct and regenerate the index if necessary.)

There are four field lines in the dialog box:

Primary Entry:
Primary Sort Key:
Secondary Entry:
Secondary Sort Key:

For Primary Entry, provide the topic under which you want Ventura to list the page number associated with this entry. If you're using See or See Also, enter the topic you are creating the cross reference for. In any case, you must provide some entry in this field to create the index entry.

For Primary Sort Key, make an entry only if you want Ventura to sort this entry according to a word different from that which will appear. Spell out a number, for example, if you want Ventura to place it alphabetically.

In Secondary Entry, provide a subtopic, if desired, under which you want Ventura to place this page reference. If you are using See or See Also, enter the topic to which you want to refer the reader.

Use the Secondary Sort Key field to specify some overriding consideration that Ventura should use for determining the order of the entry. Often, a secondary entry will begin with a preposition (*with*, *for*, and so on), but the sort should be according to the noun that follows it. Thus the Secondary Sort Key would have the same entry as Secondary Entry, but without the preposition.

When you give the OK, Ventura inserts the Index Entry mark into the document. It looks like a degree symbol (°) if you've set the Options menu to Show Tabs & Returns. When this symbol is to the right of the keyboard cursor, the words *Index Entry* appear in the Current box toward the bottom of the Side-bar. At this point, you can use Shift-Del to copy the entry and its information to the clipboard for posting on additional pages (see **Cut/Copy/Paste**).

UNDO

You can remove an index entry in either of two ways. You can cut the entry in Text mode by placing the keyboard cursor to the right of the Index Entry marker and pressing the Delete key. Alternatively, with the keyboard cursor in the same place, you can use Edit menu/Edit Special Item and delete the Primary Entry with the Esc key. (You can also use Paste to move an index entry along with the information in its dialog box; see **Cut/Copy/Paste**.)

EXAMPLE

To index Sydney under Australia, enter

```
Primary Entry: Australia
Secondary Entry: Sydney
```

To "double-post" this entry, so that Sydney has a listing as well, insert another index entry in the text such as

```
Primary Entry: Sydney (Australia)
```

You can insert this second entry right next to the first one.

To list *20/20* but place it alphabetically as if spelled out, enter

Primary Entry: 20/20
Primary Sort Key: Twenty Twenty

To direct readers searching for Sydney to look under Australia, click the See button and enter

Primary Entry: Sydney
Secondary Entry: Australia

SEE ALSO

Cut/Copy/Paste; Text

Making Entries with Headers and Footers

SEQUENCE

[create section heading]
[insert index entry in heading]
[apply tag]
[create header or footer referencing the tag]

USAGE

Use a "live" header or footer (also called a "catch phrase") to generate index entries automatically on each page in a series. Ventura uses the index entry in text (usually a section heading) with the tag you specify as the starting point. The entries appear in the headers on each page until the tag appears again, where you can replace it with a new index entry. When

Ventura generates the index, it replaces the series of individual page numbers with a span of page numbers.

In Edit mode, begin by locating or creating the section heading. (The standard text you provide for a section heading is optional. If you don't want a header or footer in the document, you can compose paragraphs that consist of nothing but the index mark and a paragraph return.) Then use the Edit menu's Insert/Edit Index dialog box to insert the index mark into the heading. Apply the appropriate tag to the heading. Then use the Page menu's Headers & Footers dialog box to create a header or footer that uses your heading tag (using the 1st Match or Last Match feature).

Provide a paragraph later that uses the same tag. You can insert a new index entry to start at that point or use the paragraph without an index entry to give Ventura an ending point for the first entry.

UNDO

To remove an entry from a header or footer, delete the index entry as described earlier. Use the Page menu's Headers & Footers dialog box to remove headers and footers, if desired.

SEE ALSO

Headers/Footers; Tags

Generating the Index

SEQUENCE OF STEPS

Options menu
Multi-Chapter
[click **Save** *if requested]*
[open or save as a publication]

Make Index
[adjust settings]
OK

USAGE

Use this procedure to generate the index, which is a publication feature (see **Publications**). Use the Options menu and select **Multi-Chapter**. If you have unsaved changes, Ventura asks whether you wish to save; choose **Save**. Then open up the publication for which you want to generate the index. (If you want an index for only one chapter file, you must save it as a publication first.) With the publication selected, select **Make Index**. In the Generate Index dialog box, you will see the default settings Ventura uses to generate the index. These settings are discussed in the following paragraphs. Once you've adjusted the settings as you desire, click **OK** to generate the index. (You cannot give the OK by using ↵, as you usually can.)

Index File is the name and directory location Ventura suggests for the text file it will generate. It uses the first five characters in the name of the publication file and adds IDX (for index) and the GEN extension (for generated).

Title String is the name Ventura will place at the top of the index file; this name is usually simply the word *Index*. This text will automatically receive the generated tag Z_INDEX TITLE.

Set Letter Headings: **On** if you want the appropriate letter of the alphabet to appear before each section of the index. The letter headings receive the tag Z_INDEX LTR.

Use the remaining field lines to indicate how Ventura should format the index's main listings. These listings receive the tag Z_INDEX MAIN.

In the TYPESET directory, the &TCHD-P1.STY sample sheet provided with Ventura has these generated tags formatted already. You can use this style sheet with the finished generated file.

The Before #s field dictates what Ventura will place before each number in the index listing. The For Each # field shows the format for a range of page numbers. Between #s indicates how you want Ventura to separate a list of successive page numbers for one index listing; After #s is for any text you want after the page numbers. You can use the "See" and "See Also" settings to change the way Ventura phrases the cross references or to provide text attributes, such as boldface.

Use the Inserts buttons to insert special codes in the field lines. Choose **Tab** to insert a Tab character (indicated by →). Choose **Chapter #** to insert the [C#] code in the index listing; in place of this code Ventura will substitute the chapter number as set by the Page menu's Chapter Counter command. (You can also simply type in the code yourself.) Click **Page #** to insert the [P#] code, which Ventura will replace with the appropriate page number. By selecting **Text Attr**, you insert the <D> code. Either click this button and replace the D with the appropriate text code or simply type in the entire bracketed code yourself. Codes are the same as those you would use to create a text attribute with a word processor (see Appendix C). For an example of field codes, see **Numbering Sections.**

UNDO

If there is a problem with a generated index, simply make your corrections and generate a new version. Ventura will ask if you want to overwrite the previous index. You cannot retrieve the overwritten version.

SEE ALSO

Page Formats; Publications; Tags; Text/Picture Files

Making Entries with Your Word Processor

SEQUENCE OF STEPS

Primary Entry only:

<$I*primary entry***>**

Primary and Secondary Entry:

<$I*primary entry;secondary entry***>**

with Sort Keys:

<$I*primary entry[primary sort key]*; *secondary entry [secondary sort key]***>**

with See cross reference:

<$S*primary entry;cross reference***>**

with See Also cross reference:

<$A*primary entry;cross reference***>**

USAGE

Use these formats to make index entries in text files with your word processor.

If available, use your word processor's macro capability to insert the appropriate symbols automatically and prompt you for the entries. You may be able to block off previously entered text and copy it to create the index entry, again assisted by a macro.

UNDO

To remove an index entry, use your word processor's procedure for deleting text. You can also use Ventura to remove index entries, as discussed above.

EXAMPLE

To index Sydney under Australia, enter

<$IAustralia;Sydney>

To list 20/20 but place it alphabetically as if spelled out, enter

<$I20/20[Twenty Twenty]>

To direct readers searching for Sydney to look under Australia, enter:

<$SSydney;Australia>

SEE ALSO

Text

Italics

You can use several methods to set text in *italics*.

VERSION

2.0, 1.1, 1.0

USAGE

You can set italics in several ways, depending on the type and extent of the materials you want to italicize. You can italicize entire paragraphs by the tag, which affects all paragraphs so tagged, or you can assign italics to individual characters within a paragraph, either with Ventura menu options or when entering text with your word processor. You can also assign italic type to special features, like big first characters; use the Set Font Properties command associated with the feature you want.

Italics with Paragraph Tags

SEQUENCE OF STEPS

Paragraph mode
[select a paragraph]
Paragraph menu
Font
Style: **Italic**
OK or ↵
[tag other paragraphs if desired]

USAGE

Using tags will make all of the characters in the selected paragraph—and all similarly tagged paragraphs—change to italics. In Paragraph mode, click a sample paragraph that you want to italicize. Use the Paragraph menu and choose **Font**. In the dialog box that appears, under the Style heading choose **Italic**. Note that Italic may not be available (as indicated by ghosting) in all faces and sizes.

UNDO

With the paragraph tagged, pull down the Paragraph menu and select **Font**. Change Style to **Normal** or some setting other than **Italic** and give the OK.

SEE ALSO

Fonts; Tags

Italicizing Selected Text

SEQUENCE OF STEPS

Text mode
[select the text]
Assignment list: **Italic**

or

Text mode,
[select the text]
Set Font button
Italic
OK or ↵

USAGE

You can italicize selected text by using the **Italic** assignment on the Side-bar or by using a font dialog box. In either case, first activate the Text mode, and then use the mouse to select the text for italics. To use the first method, you then simply click **Italic** on the Assignment list, which appears on the Side-bar when Ventura is in the Text mode. To use the second method, you then click the Set Font button; it also appears on the Side-bar in Text mode. In the dialog box that appears, under the Style heading click **Italic**. Italic may not be available in all faces and sizes.

UNDO

See the Undo instructions under "Assigning Fonts to Selected Text" in **Fonts.**

SEE ALSO

Fonts

Italics with the Word Processor

SEQUENCE

<I>*[text]***<D>**
or
[use supported word processor's italics procedure]

USAGE

If Ventura supports italics from your word processor, you can use the word processor's method for italicizing text. The text will appear in italics in Ventura and still appear in italics when you look at the text file with the word processor.

If Ventura does not support italics from your word processor, place the code **<I>** at the beginning of the text to appear in italics. Placing the code **<D>** at the end of the italics will cause the text to return to normal (as set by the paragraph tag) at that point. You can eliminate this ending code if the effect continues to the end of the paragraph because the italicizing will end when the paragraph ends unless there is another <I> code at the beginning of the next paragraph. The effect also ends when another effect begins.

UNDO

Remove the codes or effect with your word processor's delete capabilities. You can also remove the effect in Ventura using the Undo techniques given above.

EXAMPLE

The following text, imported from a word processor whose italic capability Ventura does not support:

> This is normal. <I>This is italic.<D> This is normal again.

would be printed by Ventura as

> This is normal. *This is italic.* This is normal again.

SEE ALSO

Text

Kerning

Kerning is the process of placing one letter (or other character) closer than normal to the letter that precedes it.

USAGE

Usually, Ventura does not place the leftmost part of a letter any closer than the rightmost part of the letter before it. However, with certain letter combinations, such as *W* followed by *A* or *T* followed by *o*, normal spacing can appear too loose. The larger the font, the more pronounced the effect. Kerning brings the second letter closer to the first letter. This tightens the text and makes the spacing appear normal. You can kern more than one letter simultaneously and decrease the distance between all those involved.

Ventura provides several procedures for kerning text. You can kern letters on a case-by-case basis or according to paragraph tag. You can also suspend kerning temporarily (to expedite processing) and indicate if you want kerning applied to the text on the screen as well as in print. Note that kerning differs from letter spacing and tracking, typographical effects discussed under **Spacing**.

Kerning Individual Letters

VERSION

2.0, 1.1, 1.0

SEQUENCE OF STEPS

Using the Font Setting dialog box:

Text mode
[select the letter(s)]
Side-bar's **Set Font** button
(2.0 only) Kern: **Looser** or **Tighter**
[provide a value]
OK or ↵

(2.0 only) Interactive Kerning:

Text mode
[select the letter(s)]
Shift-← or Shift-→

USAGE

This procedure brings an individual letter closer to the letter that precedes it. Because of the effort involved, you usually do this only for large-font text (headlines, for instance). The kerning you set will override kerning with a tag.

In the Text mode, use the mouse to select the letter you wish to kern. With versions 1.1 and 1.0, select the letter you want to move to the left. With version 2.0, the letter you select will pull the letter to its right closer. Then, on the Side-bar, click the **Set Font** button. You'll see a Font Setting dialog box, and an area at the bottom labeled *Kern.*

With version 2.0, you can set Kern to Looser or Tighter than the normal distance. Set as desired and then provide a value for the distance you want to kern. Before version 2.0, you provide an absolute value for kerning. With version 2.0, you provide a value for the number of ems to kern. An em is a relative amount, equal to the size of the @ symbol for the font you're using. Thus, should you change the size of your font, Ventura will adjust the kerning automatically. Give the OK and the letter will be adjusted to the left, as will the text that follows it.

In version 2.0 you can kern letters interactively. With a letter selected, hold down the Shift key and press the ← or → key. Ventura will adjust the letter following the one selected in the direction of the arrow. You may need to "re-ink" the screen with the Esc key to see the effect.

You can kern more than one letter simultaneously to decrease the distance between all those involved. Simply select the string of text and use one of the kerning techniques.

TIP

Because of the difference between screen and print fonts, a discrepancy may occur between the amount of kerning you see on the screen and the printed version. To be certain what the kerning will look like, be sure to print out a sample.

UNDO

See the Undo instructions under "Assigning Fonts to Selected Text" in **Fonts.**

SEE ALSO

Spacing; Text

EXAMPLE

In the following example, the W, A, and V are kerned to eliminate inordinate space. The E is kerned to the N for effect.

Normal text (not kerned)

NEW WAVE NEWS

NEW WAVE NEWS

Kerned text

Kerning with Tags

VERSION

2.0, 1.1

SEQUENCE OF STEPS

Paragraph mode
[select a sample paragraph]
Paragraph menu
2.0: **Paragraph Typography**; 1.1: **Typographic Controls**
Automatic Pair Kerning: **On**
OK or ↵

USAGE

Use this procedure to turn on automatic kerning, if available, for all paragraphs so tagged. The width table for the font that the tag is using must contain kerning information for the effect to work. (See **Printing.**) Also, the chapter or frame must not override this setting (see below).

In Paragraph mode, select a paragraph with the tag you wish to kern. Use the Paragraph menu and select **Typographic Controls**. In the resulting dialog box, choose Automatic Pair Kerning: **On** and give the OK.

TIP

Kerning is recommended for large fonts. Kerning with smaller fonts (10 pt. Body Text, for example) is not so necessary, but it may allow you to fit more text into a given amount of space. Tracking (see **Spacing**) also helps in this regard.

Kerning may slow down Ventura's processing time (by rewriting the screen, for instance), but read on for ways to get around this.

UNDO

With a paragraph selected, use the Paragraph menu's Paragraph Typography dialog box to set Automatic Pair Kerning: **Off**.

SEE ALSO

Spacing; Fonts; Printing

Suspending Kerning

SEQUENCE OF STEPS

To turn off kerning for the chapter:

2.0: **Chapter** menu; 1.1: **Page** menu
2.0: **Chapter Typography**; 1.1: **Page Layout**
2.0: Pair Kerning: **Off**; 1.1: Kerning: **Globally Off**
OK or ↵

To turn off kerning for a frame (2.0 only):

Frame mode or **Graphics** mode
[select the Frame]
Frame menu
Frame Typography
Pair Kerning: **Off**
OK or ↵

USAGE

Turn chapter kerning off to temporarily suspend automatic kerning for all paragraph tags. Doing so may speed up processing operations. This procedure does not change the tag's automatic kerning status (described above) but only disengages it temporarily.

Use the Chapter menu and choose **Chapter Typography**. Select Pair Kerning: **Off** to deactivate kerning for all paragraph tags. (It does not affect individual letters kerned in the Text mode.)

With version 2.0 you can override the Chapter setting on a frame-by-frame basis. With the frame selected, use Frame menu/Frame Typography. In this dialog box, Pair kerning is normally set to Default, and the frame takes its kerning cue (on or off) from the Chapter setting. Change this setting to override the chapter setting.

UNDO

With the Chapter menu, choose **Chapter Typography**. Choose Pair Kerning: **On** to reactivate kerning for tags whose Paragraph menu's Typography dialog box has Automatic Pair Kerning: On. To have a frame use the chapter's setting, select the frame and, using Frame menu/Frame Typography, set Pair Kerning to **Default.**

Screen Kerning

VERSION

2.0, 1.1

SEQUENCE OF STEPS

Options menu
Set Preferences
On-Screen Kerning: *[make setting]*
OK or ↵

USAGE

Use on-screen kerning to set the amount of kerning Ventura should perform on the screen. Less kerning can help speed up processing operations as they occur on the screen.

Use the Options menu and choose **Set Preferences** for on-screen kerning. Your options are None, 36, 24, 18, 14, 10, and All. Click **None** if you don't want Ventura to display kerning on the screen. Click one of the other buttons and on the screen Ventura will kern all text (as indicated by the tag) that is the indicated point size or higher. It will not affect individual letters kerned in Text mode.

UNDO

Using the Options menu's Set Preferences dialog box, choose On-Screen Kerning: **All** if you don't want to restrict kerning on the screen.

SEE ALSO

Fonts

Kerning with Your Word Processor

VERSION

2.0, 1.1

SEQUENCE OF STEPS

To kern using em values (2.0 only):

> **<%** *[hundredths of ems to add or subtract]***>***[text to kern]***<%0>**

To kern using units of 1/300 inch:

> **<K***[amount of displacement to the left]***>***[text to kern]***<K-001>**

USAGE

You can use your word processor to kern text. Use this method to kern individual letters (no more than one paragraph) as you would in Ventura's Text mode with the Set Font button.

To kern using em values, enter a left angle-bracket (<) and the percent symbol (%). Then provide the number of ems to kern, using negative values to kern tighter and positive values to kern looser. The text you enter will be kerned accordingly. Enter the code **<%0>** to turn off em kerning (use zero). Then continue with the rest of the text. Effects also end with with end of the paragraph or with another code.

You can also kern using absolute values. When you come to a letter that you want to shift to the left, closer to the preceding letter, enter the left angle-bracket (<), the letter K, and then a numeric value indicating kerning in 1/300ths of an inch. Close the code with a right angle-bracket (>). Then provide the letter you want shifted to the left and the code **<K-001>** to turn off the kerning (using the number zero).

UNDO

Using your word processor's delete capability, remove the codes to undo the kerning. You can also undo in Ventura as described under "Kerning Individual Letters" above.

Line Drawing

Ventura can create a variety of types of lines that are associated with other features.

VERSION

2.0, 1.1, 1.0

USAGE

You can create horizontal lines that are associated with a paragraph tag, or that are part of a frame, or vertical lines that are part of a frame (such as rules between the frame's columns). Using the Ruling Box feature, you can provide vertical lines associated with a paragraph tag. For the most flexibility, use the Graphics mode to create a variety of free-form lines and arrows.

You can also extend text lines, such as underlining, across the width of a paragraph. See **Underline/Overscore/Strike-thru.**

Horizontal Lines as Part of a Frame

SEQUENCE OF STEPS

Frame mode or also (2.0 only) **Graphics** mode
[select a frame]
Frame menu
Ruling Line Above or **Ruling Line Below**
[set width, height, other features]
OK or ↵

USAGE

Use this procedure to draw horizontal lines at the top or bottom of a frame. The lines stay with the frame, and you can have them adjust with the size of the frame automatically.

With Ventura in the Frame mode, select a frame at the top or bottom of which you want to place up to three lines. Use the Frame menu and select **Ruling Line Above** or **Below**. In the dialog box that appears, choose Width: **Frame** (the only width, besides None, available for frames). Set the Color and Pattern as desired. (For a chart of the patterns, see **Graphics**.) White lines will not show unless they're against a dark background (which you can set with the Frame menu's Frame Background dialog box).

Starting with Rule 1, set the Height (thickness) of up to 3 lines. Set the space between the lines. The Space Below Rule 3 setting does not apply to Ruling Lines Above, and the Space Above Rule 1 setting does not apply to Ruling Lines Below (see Figure 25). As you provide these settings, samples of the lines will appear in the dialog box. However, the sample (including the spacing) is twice the size that it appears in the document. Only the first half-inch of lines appear in the sample. Thus, if your settings are more than one-half inch, the sample may not appear (though the document will be affected nonetheless). You cannot change the size of the display; it always displays the first half-inch. The Overall Height indicator displays the total of the values set above it. Thus it indicates the total thickness of the lines and spacing.

To create a line composed of dashes, select Dashes: **On**. Then provide values for Dash Width (length) and Dash Spacing (the distance between dashes). Other settings (Custom Indent, Custom Width) don't apply in the Frame mode.

To be sure that text or other material that appears within a frame does not conflict with the frame's ruling lines, you must provide the frame with margins great enough to accommodate the lines. Ventura will not allow the frame's text within those margins. Use the Frame menu's Margins & Columns dialog box to adjust the margins (see **Margins**).

UNDO

With the frame selected, use the Frame menu and choose **Ruling Line Above** or **Ruling Line Below**. For Width, select **None** and give the OK.

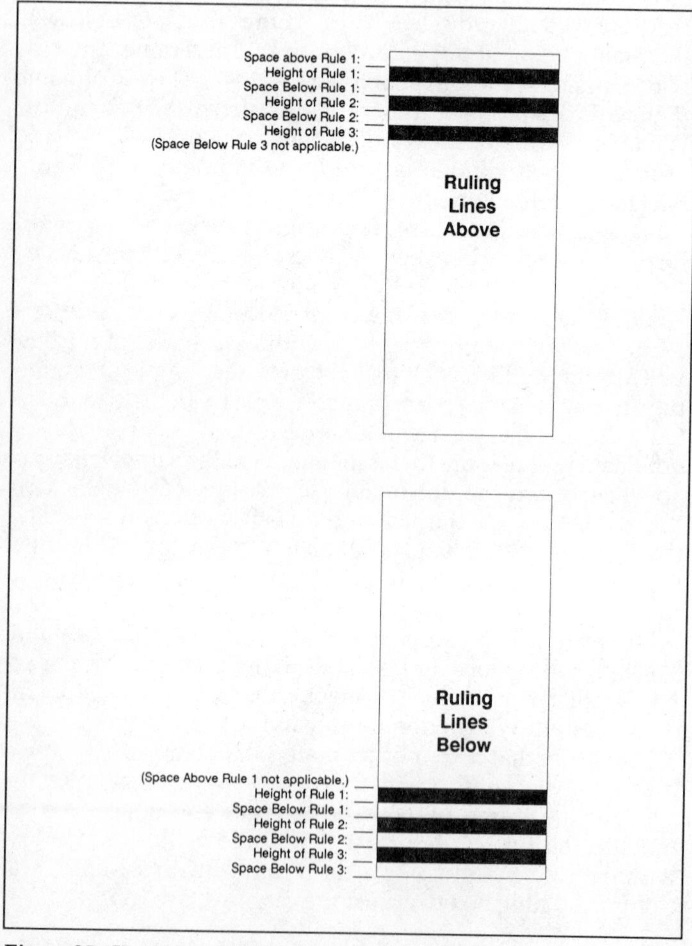

Figure 25: Horizontal line measurements for frames

SEE ALSO

Boxes; Frames; Margins

Horizontal Lines Associated with Paragraph Tags

SEQUENCE OF STEPS

Paragraph mode
[select a paragraph]
Paragraph menu
Ruling Line Above *or* **Ruling Line Below**
[set width, height, other features]
OK or ↵
[tag other paragraphs if desired]

USAGE

This technique assigns horizontal ruling lines by the paragraph tag. All paragraphs so tagged will be ruled. In Paragraph mode, select a sample paragraph. Use the Paragraph menu and select **Ruling Line Above** or **Ruling Line Below**. In the resulting dialog box, set the features discussed under "Horizontal Lines as Part of a Frame."

Other parts of the dialog box, ghosting in Frame mode, become available in Paragraph mode. Under Width, choose **Text** if you want the lines to be the same width as the text of the paragraphs. (For Ruling Lines Above, Ventura matches the length with that of the first line of the paragraph. For Ruling Lines Below, it uses the last line of text.) Select **Margin** to set the box according to the paragraph's In From Left and In From Right values (set by the Paragraph menu's Spacing dialog box).

By choosing **Custom** you can provide a value for Custom Width and so set the length of the line without restriction.

Then, optionally, you can provide a value for Custom Indent. This value will offset the left edge of the line in from the left edge of the paragraph. To create an outdented line instead, click the **Minus** (–) button.

UNDO

With the paragraph selected, use the Paragraph menu and select **Ruling Line Above** or **Ruling Line Below** as appropriate. For Width, select **None** and give the OK.

SEE ALSO

Tags; Breaking Paragraphs

Column Rules and Other Vertical Frame Lines

SEQUENCE OF STEPS

Frame mode or also (2.0 only) **Graphics** mode
[select frame]
Frame menu
Vertical Rules
[adjust settings]
OK or ↵

USAGE

Use the Vertical Rules dialog box to create ruling lines that are associated with a frame. Creating these lines for the underlying-page frame causes them to appear on each similar page (see **Page Formats**).

Activate the Frame mode (or Graphics mode in 2.0) and click the frame that you want the vertical lines associated with. Use the Frame menu and choose **Vertical Rules**. In the Vertical Rules dialog box, you'll see two Settings For buttons, Left Page and Right Page. You can use these buttons to create different sets of lines on double-sided pages. With single-sided pages, this dialog box will display the settings that correspond to the only page side in use, indicated in the Current box.

Use Inter-Col Rules to create lines between columns. Choose **On** and provide a value for Width, the thickness of the line(s). Column rules will appear only if you've used the Frame menu's Margins & Columns dialog box on the same frame to specify multiple columns and to provide a gutter between the columns to accommodate the line (see **Columns**).

Use the Rule 1 and Rule 2 settings to create one or two vertical bars that appear within the selected frame but whose position is measured from the left edge of the page (regardless of the frame). Column-wide text will not flow around these rules automatically. To keep text away from the rule, use the Frame menu's Margins & Columns dialog box (to make a text-free margin) or use the Paragraph menu's Alignment menu (to change a tag's Overall Width to Frame-Wide) or use the Paragraph menu's Spacing dialog box (to increase a tag's In From Left or In From Right value).

With double-sided pages, you can duplicate your settings for one side on the other side. Select the **Copy To Facing Page** button at the bottom of the Vertical Rules dialog box. Settings are copied exactly, not mirrored.

UNDO

In Frame mode with the frame selected, use the Vertical Rules dialog box. To remove lines between columns, choose Inter-Col Rules: **Off**. To remove vertical page bars, set Rule 1 Width and Rule 2 Width to 0 (you can use the Esc key). With double-sided pages, remove lines for one side and then click **Copy To Facing Page**.

EXAMPLE

See Figure 26.

SEE ALSO

Margins; Spacing; Tags

Vertical Lines with Paragraph Tags

SEQUENCE OF STEPS

Paragraph mode
[select a paragraph]
Paragraph menu
Ruling Box Around
Width: **Custom**
[provide an identical value for Custom Width and Height Of Rule 1]
[optionally provide a value for Custom Indent]
OK or ↵
[tag other paragraphs if desired]

USAGE

When you create a vertical bar associated with a paragraph tag, the length of the bar automatically adjusts to match the amount of text in each paragraph so tagged. This effect is often used to create a *change bar*, a line to the left of text indicating that changes have been made to that paragraph.

In Paragraph mode, select a paragraph with the tag you want for this effect. Then use the Paragraph menu and choose **Ruling Box Around**. Select Width: **Custom** and provide an identical value for Custom Width and Height Of Rule 1. This will determine the thickness of the line.

Custom Indent positions the bar from the left edge of the paragraph to the right edge of the bar. With Custom Indent at zero, the bar is immediately to the left of the paragraph. To provide some space between the bar and the text, give this setting a small negative value (click the **Minus** button). To position the bar to the right of the text, provide a positive value for Custom Indent at least as great as the width of the paragraph plus the width of the bar. (You can use the rulers to determine the width; see **Rulers**.)

UNDO

With the paragraph selected, use the Paragraph menu's Ruling Box Around dialog box. Set width to **None** to remove a tag's vertical line.

CD-ROM Breaks New Ground

Compact Disk Read Only Memory (CD-ROM) is a rapidly emerging new technology for the retrieval of vast amounts of information from an optical disk. This new peripheral device allows a totally new level of functionality in the use of microcomputers.

Physically, the CD-ROM device has a laser disk drive (or "player") the same size as a traditional 5 1/4" drive. The removable disk is 4 3/4", and has a capacity of 550M bytes (equivalent to 1500 360K floppy disks).

Theory of Operation

Information stored on a CD-ROM can be loaded into memory (RAM), displayed and printed, as with other media. While that data in RAM may be altered and stored to a conventional magnetic disk, the original information on the CD-ROM is unalterable, always ensuring the original copy is intact, making archiving easy.

The storage capacity, low cost, and read only feature of CD-ROM bring an enormous new capability to microcomputer users – that is, information retrieval of very large reference publications. How people receive and use information in the immediate and long term future will be dramatically changed by CD-ROM.

In addition to the huge capacity of raw information storage, specialized software for the search of that information is currently being introduced. This software allows searching the information in areas, methods and speeds not previously feasible.

It now becomes possible to electronically publish reference material more

Figure 26: Column rules

EXAMPLE

The Adventure Begins 3

ried us on our hour and fifteen minute, 66 kilometer trip into the center of the city and the Imperial Hotel. Much of the super highway into town is screened by noise abating walls. Traffic moves steadily at about 50 miles an hour and we observed no speeding. The new Imperial Hotel is every bit as good as its reputation—somewhat more elegant than the Ritz Carlton. Our room in the new tower looks exactly like the picture in the travel folders. It's not exceptionally large. It has a bay window overlooking the Ginza with the ocean in the background, very nice furniture, and a well-appointed onyx and plastic bathroom.

"Extras" abound: Toothbrushes, terrycloth bathrobes, kimonos, slippers, coffee making equipment, etc. There are eleven separate restaurants in the hotel, all—as we have found by inspection (reading the menus that is) very expensive. To settle later discussion by the way, the price of our room is 34,000 Yen per day plus 10% gratuities and 10% on the whole thing.

SEE ALSO

Boxes; Spacing; Tags

Graphics Lines

SEQUENCE OF STEPS

(1.1 and 1.0 only) **Frame** mode
[select associated frame]
Graphics mode
[click line icon]
[drag mouse to draw line]

USAGE

Use the Graphics mode to draw lines in a more free-form manner. In Frame mode (or also Graphics mode in 2.0), choose the frame that you want the line to be tied to. Then switch to Graphics mode if necessary. Click the **Line** icon:

to create a line. You can then set the attributes for the line; use the Graphics menu's Line Attributes dialog box to add an arrowhead, for example (see **Graphics**).

UNDO

In the Graphics mode, select the line. Then press the Delete key or use the Edit menu and select **Cut Graphic**.

SEE ALSO

Frames; Graphics

Margins

Ventura can set margins for the page or within a frame.

VERSION

SEQUENCE OF STEPS

Frame mode or also (2.0 only) **Graphics** mode
[select a frame]
Frame menu
Margins & Columns
[adjust Margins settings]
OK or ↵

USAGE

To set margins for the page, use the underlying-page frame, which will affect all similar pages (see **Page Formats**).

In the Frame mode, select the frame within which you want to adjust the margins. Use the Frame menu and choose **Margins & Columns**. In the dialog box that appears, under Margins you'll see Top, Bottom, Left, and Right. Provide the values for the width of these margins from the edges of the frame to the text or picture within. (In the case of the underlying-page frame, these are distances from the edge of the paper.)

For double-sided pages, the settings are initially for the displayed page, as indicated by the Settings For button. Click the opposite button (Left Page or Right Page) to adjust the settings for the opposite page or click **Copy To Facing Page** to have Ventura reflect the margins on the opposite page. For binding facing pages, use Copy To Facing Page to create wide inside margins on the underlying-page frame.

Note that margins restrict text and pictures that appear *within* a frame. To control the space that *surrounds* a frame, use frame padding (see **Frames**).

UNDO

In Frame mode, select the frame from which you want to remove the margins. Then use the Frame menu's Margins & Columns dialog box and use the Esc key to set the Top, Bottom, Left, and Right margins to zero.

SEE ALSO

Frames; Page Formats

Mouse Operations

The mouse is an important input tool in working with Ventura; you can use it to make selections and initiate actions with practically all of the program's features.

VERSION

2.0, 1.1, 1.0

SEQUENCE OF STEPS

To select a button, frame, graphic, paragraph:

[click the item]

To position the keyboard cursor in text:

[click text position]

To display a drop-down menu (all Options):

[point to menu name]

To select a block of text:

[position cursor at beginning of block, drag to end, release]

To select and OK a file in an Item Selection box:

[double-click the file name]

To see an item on a pop-up menu:

[point to the current selection and press]

To select an item on a pop-up menu:

[drag to the item and release]

USAGE

In Ventura, as you move the mouse, a corresponding indicator, called the mouse cursor, moves on the screen. It can take on a variety of shapes, depending on the current operation (see Figure 27).

By moving the mouse and using the mouse button, you can effect a variety of operations in Ventura. Use the mouse to click buttons on the Side-bar and in dialog boxes, to place the keyboard cursor in text, to display menus and select items that appear, and to select text, frames, paragraphs, and

MOUSE CURSOR SHAPES	MODE	OPERATION
+	Frame	
FR	·	Add new frame
		Resize frame
		Crop image
		Move frame
	Paragraph	
I	Text	
	Graphic	
Te		Box text
		Line drawing
⊕		Circle drawing
		Rectangle drawing
		Rounded rectangle drawing

Note: The mouse cursor changes to ↖ when you make selections from pull-down menus, dialog boxes, and the Side-bar.

Figure 27: Mouse cursor shapes

graphics. If your mouse has more than one button, Ventura only uses the left one. Here are some operations you can perform with the mouse:

- Position or Point: Place the mouse at a certain location on the screen. Pointing may cause some change on the screen, such as the display of a menu.
- Click: Press the mouse button and quickly release it while pointing at a button, icon, menu item and so on.

You can change Ventura's operating mode by clicking one of the four mode buttons at the top of the Side-bar.

- Double-click: Press and release the mouse button twice in rapid succession. In an Item Selector box, you can select a file by clicking it; you can both select it and give the OK by double-clicking the file name.
- Drag: Position the cursor at a particular location and press and hold the mouse button. Then, while still holding the button, move the mouse to another location. You can use this procedure to select text, draw graphics, or to display and choose from a pop-up menu (version 2.0 only) in the dialog boxes.
- Release: Let go of the mouse button. After dragging the mouse to a certain location, you release it to indicate the ending position of a defined area.
- Press or Depress: Press the button on the mouse and hold. You can see the alternatives available for items with pop-up menus by positioning the mouse on the current selection and pressing.

You can use the keyboard in conjunction with the mouse. Use the following keys to perform the operations indicated by holding down the indicated key while you click or otherwise use the mouse:

- Alt: Crops pictures as you drag on the picture. With version 2.0, constrains graphics (for example, draws squares, not rectangles; circles, not ellipses) when you draw them initially or change them.
- Ctrl: Selects hidden frames or graphics as you click them in the working area.
- Shift: Selects multiple frames or graphics as you click them in the working area. Selects the text from the keyboard cursor to the indicated position. Allows you to add multiple frames or graphics by keeping the Add button operational.

Moving Frames, Text, Graphics

Moving frames to another page, see **Cut/Copy/Paste**.
Relocating frame on the same page, see **Frames**.
Moving text or graphics, see **Cut/Copy/Paste**.

Moving within a Document

With Ventura, you can display any given page of the document, in relative or absolute terms.

VERSION

2.0, 1.1, 1.0

Moving Relative to the Document

SEQUENCE OF STEPS

Using the Go To Page dialog box:

Ctrl-G or **Chapter** menu/**Go To Page**
Relative To: **Document**
Which Page: **First** or **Prev** or **Selected** or **Next** or **Last**

[if "Selected," provide selected page number]
OK or ↵

Using the shortcut keys:

Home key: First page of the document
End key: Last page of the document
PgDn key: Next page of the document
PgUp key: Prev page of the document

USAGE

Use these procedures to display a different page in the document from the one you are currently viewing. To use the Go To Page dialog box, either type Ctrl-G or pull down the Chapter menu (Page menu in versions 1.1 and 1.0) and choose **Go To Page**. In the Which Page grouping, Selected is initially chosen, which allows you to specify a page number to go to. The Current Page indicator shows the number of the page that was on display before you invoked the dialog box. Initially, the number for Selected Page is the same as this number. Edit the Selected Page number (Esc to remove the number) and show the number of the page you want to display. Click OK or press ↵. For Which Page, you can also choose **First**, **Prev**, **Next**, or **Last**, but to go to these pages in the document, it's easier to use the shortcut keys. Press the Home key to immediately display the first page of the document, press End to display the last page, and press PgDn and PgUp to display the next and previous page, respectively.

UNDO

Use the Go To Page dialog box or the opposite shortcut key to go back to the page you were on.

Moving Relative to a File

SEQUENCE OF STEPS

[select a frame with a text file]
Ctrl-G or **Chapter** menu/**Go To Page**
Relative To: **File**
Which Page: **First** or **Prev** or **Selected** or **Next** or **Last**
[if "Selected," provide selected page number]
OK or ↵

USAGE

Use this procedure to follow text from one frame that holds it to the next one it appears in. First, you must select the frame that the text is in. Then press Ctrl-G or, using the Chapter menu (Page menu in 1.1 and 1.0), select **Go To Page**. Ventura will display Relative To: File (instead of Relative To: Document). For Which Page, specify **First**, **Prev**, **Next**, or **Last** and then click OK or press ↵. Ventura will display the page that contains the text of the selected frame. You can also specify a selected page as above.

If you specify a page that does not contain the file in the frame, Ventura will display the next page that does. If the page you indicate is after the last page with the file, Ventura will display the last page with the file.

Numbering Adjustments

You can reset an automatic figure or table number for a caption label.

VERSION

2.0, 1.1, 1.0

SEQUENCE OF STEPS

Version 2.0:

[in Frame mode, select caption frame or host frame if you're adjusting the counter for a particular frame]
Chapter menu
Update Counters
Chapter or **This Page** or **This Table** or **This Figure** or **Initial Page** or **Initial Table** or **Initial Figure**
[adjust other settings in the dialog box]
OK or ↵

Before version 2.0, you adjust counters through separate dialog boxes:

Figure counter: **Frame** mode, **Frame** menu, **Figure Counter**
Table counter: **Frame** mode, **Frame** menu, **Table Counter**
Chapter counter: (Any mode) **Page** menu, **Chapter Counter**
Page counter: (Any mode) **Page** menu, **Page Counter**

USAGE

Use this procedure to reset an automatic figure or table number for a caption label. All automatically numbered captions that follow this caption will be adjusted. You can also adjust the numbering/lettering format.

To adjust a figure or table number after creating the caption with the [F#] or [T#] code, use the Frame mode and select the caption frame or its host frame. On the Chapter menu, select **Update Counters**. In the dialog box that appears, choose **This Table** or **This Figure**, as appropriate, then choose **Restart Number** and provide a number.

Choose one of the settings in the Number Format grouping to set the style of numbering. Arabic or roman numerals, upper- or lowercase letters, or spelled-out numbers are available. Captions that follow this frame will change in style as well.

With version 2.0, you can also use this dialog box (in any mode of Ventura) to set the number of the first figure or table in the chapter. Click **Initial Figure** or **Initial Table** and adjust the settings. Use this if you need to make the document pick up numbering from some previously published material. If the last figure was 24, you could use Initial Figure to start with 25.

You can also change the chapter number (usually 1) for the entire chapter as it appears when you use the [C#] code (double-numbering of figures, such as 2.1, 2.2, 2.3, and so on). Click **Chapter**, then enter a different number. Use this ability when you need to adjust the chapter number so it picks up where pre-published material left off.

With version 2.0, you can also insert the chapter or page number anywhere in text. In Text mode, place the text cursor where you want to insert the number. Then use Edit menu/Ins Special Item (or press **Ctrl-C**). In the dialog box that appears, click **Cross-Ref** (or press **F6**). Then click **Page #** (or press ↵) or **Chapter #**, and Ventura will insert the appropriate number in the text. You can change such references with Edit menu/Edit Special Item (or **Ctrl-D**).

With version 2.0, you can also carry chapter, figure, table, and page numbering forward automatically from one chapter to another. Print the chapters in sequence as a publication (see **Publications**).

The chapters must be linked as a publictaion. Use Option menu/Multi-Chapter Operations to open the publication and then click **Renumber.**

UNDO

With the frame in which numbering restarts selected, use the Chapter menu and choose **Update Counters**. Click the **Which Counter** button corresponding to the counter you wish to increment normally and then click the Previous Number + 1 button. (Before version 2.0, use the dialog box listed under Sequence above and choose Restart Counting: **No**.)

For example, assume you had the Initial Figure of the chapter set to begin with 5 for the figure number. To have the initial figure begin with 1 again, click Initial Figure, then click the Previous Number + 1 button.

SEE ALSO

Publications

Numbering Sections

Ventura can automatically number (label) sections and subsections within a chapter.

VERSION

2.0, 1.1, 1.0

Creating Section Labels

SEQUENCE OF STEPS

(2.0) **Chapter** menu or (1.1) **Page** menu
Auto-Numbering
Usage: **On**
[fill in Level fields]
OK or ↵

USAGE

Use this procedure to automatically provide labels, consisting of repeated text and variable inserts, before paragraphs with specified tags. The variable inserts allow you to precede text with automatic numbers. You can number sections within sections, up to ten levels deep. The settings you provide are stored with the style sheet and apply to any chapter to which the style sheet is attached.

Use the Chapter menu (Page menu in 1.1) and choose **Auto-Numbering**. In the Auto-Numbering dialog box, click Usage: **On** to activate the auto-numbering system.

Next, in the dialog box provide the fields, Level 1 through Level 10, with coded entries to create the numbering. Entries can be a combination of standard text and variable inserts. The Insert grouping consists of eight buttons. Click a button to insert a code in the Level field that has the keyboard cursor at the time:

INSERT BUTTON	INSERTED CODE
Chapter #	[C#]
1,2	[*tag name,1]
A,B	[*tag name,A]
a,b	[*tag name,a]
I,II	[*tag name,I]

i,ii	[*tag name,i]
Suppress Previous Level	[-]
Text Attr	<D>

To create a label consisting of a number only, first click the button that corresponds to the numbering system you want. Next, delete the words *tag name* and replace them with the actual name of the tag you want Ventura to use to determine and number the Level 1 paragraphs. Alternatively, rather than clicking buttons and replacing text, you could simply type in the entire entry yourself. Using the buttons, though, ensures the proper syntax.

Click OK or press ↵. In front of all paragraphs with the specified tag, Ventura enters numbers in ascending sequence starting with 1 (assuming you've chosen the **1,2** style). The generated number is in its own paragraph, separated (with a return) from the Chapter Head paragraph it precedes. Ventura tags this generated paragraph with the generated tag Z_SEC1. Each label receives a generated tag that begins with Z_SEC and then indicates the tag's level. By clicking the label and using the Paragraph menu, you can adjust the label's tag attributes. You can place the generated label on the same line as the text it precedes by adjusting the breaks (see **Breaking Paragraphs**).

You can add text to the section labels as well. In the Auto-Numbering dialog box, type in the text outside of the brackets—before, after, or between coded entries.

You can click the Chapter # button to insert the [C#] code, which inserts the current chapter number, as set with Chapter menu/Update Counters (see **Numbering Adjustments**). You can click the Text Attr button to insert the <D> code, which you edit by removing the D and replacing it with text attribute codes, like those you'd use when entering text with a word processor (see Appendix C). You can also use the Alt key in conjunction with the keypad to enter special character codes (also in Appendix C).

With Level 2 and lower, Ventura normally includes the previous level as part of the numbering system. You can eliminate previous-level labels by clicking the Suppress Previous Level button, usually at the end of the label line.

UNDO

Use the Chapter menu and select **Auto-Numbering**. Click Usage: **Off** and give the OK. The entries on the fields will ghost, allowing them to become available again should you later set Usage: **On**.

EXAMPLE

Suppose that before each paragraph with the Section Head tag you want to place a bullet, then the word *Part*, followed by a space, the chapter number, a comma, and a space. Then you want the word *Section*, followed by a space and, in italics, a capital letter for the section. After this letter, you want a colon to separate the label from the text that will follow it.

1. Type **Alt-195** for the bullet, then a space, the word **Part**, and another space. Then click the **Chapter #** button, type a comma, and a space.
2. Type **Section**, a space, click the **Text Attr** button, and edit in **I** for italics.
3. Click the **A,B** button, edit in the tag name **Section Head**, and type a colon.

The result on the field line will look like this:

- **Part [C#], Section <I>[*Section Head, A]:**

The result for the A section of Part 1 will be printed as follows:

- Part 1, Section *A*:

SEE ALSO

Numbering Adjustments; Tags

Renumbering Sections

SEQUENCE OF STEPS

(2.0) **Chapter** menu or (1.1, 1.0) **Page** menu
Renumber Chapter

or

Ctrl-B

USAGE

Use this procedure to renumber sections that make use of the Chapter menu's Auto-Numbering. This will be necessary if you edit material, such as removing a section head.

Use the Chapter menu (Page menu before version 2.0) and select **Renumber Chapter**. Alternatively, simply press **Ctrl-B**. Ventura will scan the document and renumber it according to the level labels you've provided.

UNDO

Ventura provides no direct method of returning the document to its condition before renumbering, so you should save the document before performing this procedure. Then, should you obtain undesirable results, you can use File menu/Abandon to retrieve the saved version from the disk.

Options

The Options menu allows you to customize Ventura's *user interface,* the manner in which Ventura presents itself and operates for you.

VERSION

2.0, 1.1, 1.0

SEQUENCE OF STEPS

Options menu

USAGE

There are four sections to the Options menu, and our discussion is grouped accordingly. Since the Options operate in conjunction with other features, most are discussed elsewhere in this book in the context of those features. Cross-references in the following sections refer you to those features.

First Section: Options-setting Dialog Boxes

SEQUENCE OF STEPS

Options menu
Set Preferences or **Set Ruler** or **Set Printer Info** or **Add/Remove Fonts**

USAGE

The first section of the Options menu leads to four dialog boxes that allow you to set options: Set Preferences, Set Ruler, Set Printer Info, and Add/Remove Fonts.

Set Preferences Use the Options menu to display the Set Preferences dialog box. This dialog box offers the following settings. For a discussion of a particular option, see the topic indicated.

SETTING	OPTIONS	SEE
Generated Tags	Hidden Shown	Tags
Text to Greek	None 2 thru 10 All	View Changes
Keep Backup Files	Yes No	Chapters
Double Click Speed	Slow 2, 3, 4 Fast	Appendix B
On-Screen Kerning	None 36, 24, 18, 14, 10 All	Kerning
Auto-Adjustments	None Styles " and -- Both	Fonts, Text
Pop-Up Menu Symbol	Hidden Shown	Appendix B
Menu Type	Drop-Down Pull-Down	Appendix B
Decimal Tab Character	(field)	Tables

Adjust the setting as desired and register your choices by clicking OK or pressing ↵.

Other Dialog Boxes For a discussion of the other dialog boxes that spring from the first section of the Options menu, see the topics indicated.

OPTION	SEE
Set Ruler	Rulers
Set Printer Info	Printing
Add/Remove Fonts	Fonts

UNDO

Use the Options menu and redisplay the appropriate dialog box. Adjust the desired setting and give the OK.

Second Section: Hide/Show

SEQUENCE OF STEPS

Options Menu
Hide (feature) or **Show** (feature)

USAGE

Use the options in this section to show (display) or hide (make to disappear) features and codes from the Ventura screen. When you choose one of these settings, it toggles (changes) to its opposite. For instance, if the Side-bar were showing and you used **Hide Side-bar**, the Side-bar would disappear and you would see *Show Side-bar* the next time you looked at the Options menu. These settings carry over from one Ventura session to the next (see Appendix A).

Two of these have Ctrl key shortcuts, as indicated below and on the Options menu. You can use the shortcuts in place of the Options menu.

Hide/Show Side-bar (Ctrl-W) Removes or displays the Side-bar on the left side of the screen, to provide more room for editing or to make the settings on the Side-bar available for use. See Appendix B.

Hide/Show Rulers Removes or displays the rulers at the top and left of the working area to provide more room for editing or to allow you to use the rulers. See **Rulers**.

Hide/Show Column Guides Removes or displays light dashes that indicate the positions of columns, as set for the underlying-page frame. See **Columns**.

Hide/Show All/This Picture(s) Removes or displays pictures to increase the speed of editing and printing operations or so you can see the pictures. This option operates on This Picture for the last selected picture or All Pictures when the underlying-page frame or no picture frame is selected in the Frame mode. See **Pictures**.

Hide/Show Tabs and Returns (Ctrl-T) Removes or displays various screen codes (that don't appear in the printed version of your document) so you can see an accurate representation of the printed document or be aware of the codes' positions. See Appendix C.

Hide/Show Loose Lines Removes or displays the reverse video indication of loose lines (which doesn't show when printed) to represent accurately the printed version or to aid in tightening these lines. See **Spacing**.

UNDO

Use the Options menu and select the opposite, **Show** or **Hide**, as appropriate, or use the keyboard shortcut if available.

Third Section: Turn Snaps On/Off

SEQUENCE OF STEPS

Options menu
Turn Column Snap or **Line Snap On** or **Off**

USAGE

Use these options to activate or deactivate Ventura's column snap or line snap features. These features allow you to align frames precisely—to match the frames' edges to the columns and to the lines of body text that make up the underlying-page frame—as you create or adjust the frames (see **Frames**).

Use the Options menu and choose the applicable option. Once you do, the snap effect will turn on or off, and the listed option will switch to its opposite setting (On or Off). Normally, these features are turned off.

UNDO

Use the Options menu and click the same option to switch the effect again.

Fourth Section: Multi-Chapter

SEQUENCE OF STEPS

Options menu
Multi-Chapter

USAGE

This option leads you to multi-chapter features for use in creating publications. These features are discussed under **Publications, Indexing,** and **Table of Contents.**

UNDO

In the Multi-Chapter dialog box, click the **Done** button or press ↵.

Orphans

See **Widows/Orphans**.

Overscore

See **Underline/Overscore/Strike-thru**.

Page Formats

Ventura allows you to specify the size and orientation of the page you use and to add and remove pages and adjust page numbering.

VERSION

2.0, 1.1, 1.0

Page Layouts

SEQUENCE OF STEPS

(2.0) **Chapter** menu; (1.1, 1.0) **Page** menu
Page Size & Layout
[adjust settings]
OK or ↵

USAGE

Use the Page Layout dialog box to adjust settings in advance for the paper you will be using for your document. You do not actually have to use the size of paper you specify for your document; if necessary, Ventura will allow you to make compensating adjustments with a frame or when you print (see **Printing**).

To display the Page Layout dialog box, use the Chapter menu (1.1 and 1.0: Page menu) and choose Page Size & Layout. In the dialog box, set Orientation to the direction you will be using the paper: Portrait (vertical) or Landscape (horizontal).

Set Paper Type & Dimension to one of the sizes available:

Half	5.5 x 8.5 in.
Letter	8.5 x 11 in.
Legal	8.5 x 14 in.
Double	11 x 17 in.
B5	17.6 x 25 cm.
A4	21 x 29.7 cm.
Broad Sheet	18 x 24 in.

If none of these dimensions suits the paper size you desire, use the next larger size. Then decrease the size of the underlying-page frame with the Frame menu's Sizing and Scaling dialog box (see **Frames**).

Set Sides to Single or Double, depending on whether you will be printing for a single- or double-sided document. Set Starts On to Left Side or Right Side, depending on the side you want Ventura to assign to the first page in the document. This assignment appears in the Current box toward the bottom of the Side-bar. For double-sided documents, Ventura will alternate the page assignments. For single-sided documents, all pages will receive the designation you specify.

TIP

For both single- and double-sided documents, the side showing will be governed in the various dialog boxes by the matching side. Table 2 shows the dialog boxes influenced by the settings you assign to Sides and Starts On.

MENU	MENU CHOICE	SETTING
File	To Print	Which Pages
View	Facing Pages View	
Chapter (2.0) or Page (1.0, 1.1)	Page Size & Layout	Sides Starts On
	Headers & Footers	Define Inserts
Frame	Margins & Columns	Settings For Inserts
	Repeating Frame	For All Pages
	Vertical Rules	Settings For Inserts
Paragraph	Spacing	Inserts
	Breaks	Page Break

Table 2: Settings affected by the Page Layout dialog box

UNDO

Use the same procedure to display the Page Layout dialog box. Readjust the settings and give the OK.

EXAMPLE

To print on a standard, 8-1/2 by 11 inch sheet of paper in the normal upright direction, use the settings Orientation: **Portrait** and Paper Type & Dimension: **Letter, 8.5 x 11 in**. To set up a double-sided document that begins on the right side (the convention), use Sides: **Double**, Starts On: **Right Side**.

SEE ALSO

Printing

Adding and Removing Pages

SEQUENCE OF STEPS

(2.0) **Chapter** menu; (1.1, 1.0) **Page** menu
Insert/Remove Page
[select Operation]
OK or ↵

USAGE

Use this procedure to insert or remove pages from a document. When you insert a page, you can place it before or after the page showing when you initiate the procedure. When you remove a page, you remove the page showing.

Display the appropriate page in the document (see **Moving Within a Document**). Then use the Chapter menu (1.1 and 1.0: Page menu) and choose Insert / Remove Page. For Operation, click one of the choices you see displayed:

Insert New Page Before Current Page
Insert New Page After Current Page *(the default)*
Remove Current Page

Then click **OK** or press ↵.

TIP

When you assign a file to an underlying-page frame (see **Text /Picture Files**), Ventura generates as many pages as necessary to accommodate all the text in the file. When you use this procedure to insert a new page, that page initially has the same underlying-frame attributes (margins, columns, rules, background) as the page that comes before it in the chapter. However, by inserting a page like this, you create a new underlying-page frame. Should a text file you assign to the new page run longer than one page, Ventura will generate additional pages to accommodate the file. These pages will share the attributes of the new page and will adjust as you adjust the attributes of any one page. Previously created or generated pages will adjust with their generated pages (see Figure 28).

UNDO

To remove a newly inserted page, go to the page you want to remove and use the same dialog box to remove the page. You cannot remove an automatically generated page: Ventura will simply generate it again. Instead, you must remove the assigned text file (see **Text/Picture Files**) and then remove the generated pages, one by one. You cannot restore a removed page.

EXAMPLE

Assuming that page 5 is displayed in the working area, consider three scenarios: (1) Using Insert New Page Before Current Page would create a new page 5 that would initially share the attributes of page 4. The old page 5 would become page 6. (2) Using Insert New Page After Current Page would create a new page 6 that would share the attributes of the existing page 5. (3) Using Remove Current Page would remove the existing page 5 from the document and page 6 would become page 5.

SEE ALSO

Frames

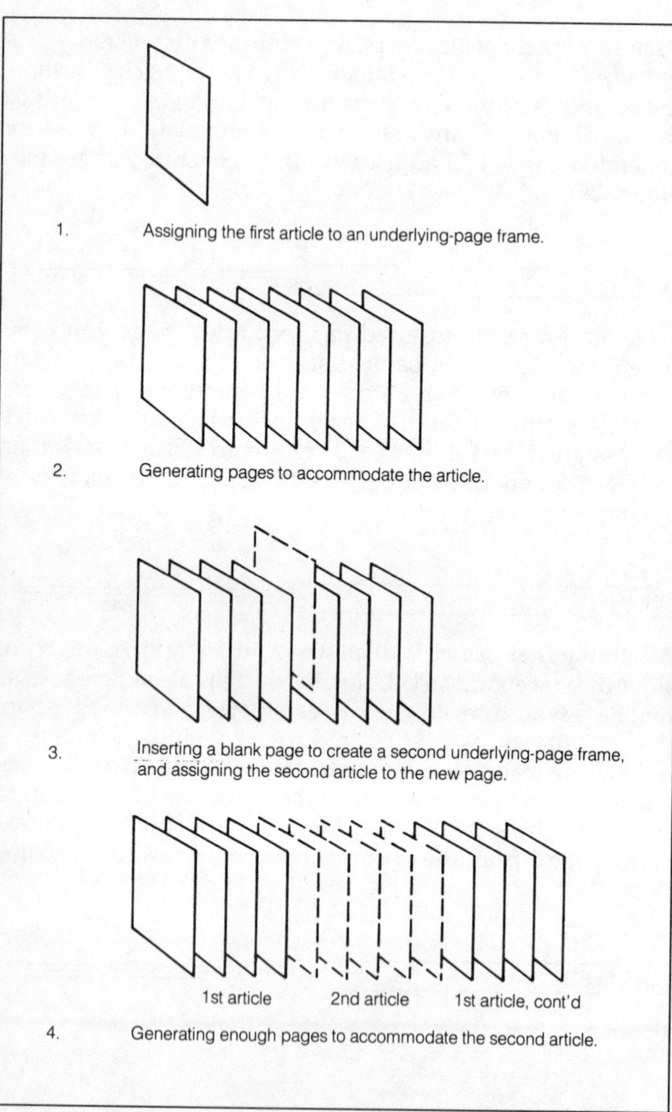

1. Assigning the first article to an underlying-page frame.
2. Generating pages to accommodate the article.
3. Inserting a blank page to create a second underlying-page frame, and assigning the second article to the new page.
1st article
2nd article
1st article, cont'd
4. Generating enough pages to accommodate the second article.

Figure 28: Inserting a page to create a second underlying-page frame

Generating Pages Automatically

SEQUENCE OF STEPS

[in Text mode, click underlying-page frame to display End of File mark (□)]
[place frames to fill up the entire page]

USAGE

When you assign a text file to an underlying-page frame, Ventura automatically generates enough pages to display the entire file. For some applications, however, you do not assign a file to the underlying-page frame but instead fill the entire page with frames.

To create additional pages, you can use the procedures described in "Adding and Renaming Pages" to insert a new page. If you do, however, the new page will have a new underlying-page frame. As such, changes you make to one page will not take effect on other pages.

If you want the pages to adjust together, you can have Ventura automatically generate additional pages, as shown in Figure 29. First, using the Text mode, click the empty underlying-page frame. (Before version 2.0, Ventura will ask you to assign a file name.) This will cause Ventura to display the End of File mark (□). Fill the page with the frames that lay out the page. (It is not necessary to fill the page's margins with frames.) When frames fill the page, Ventura will generate a new page to hold the End of File mark. Fill as many pages with frames as necessary to create the document.

EXAMPLE

See Figure 29.

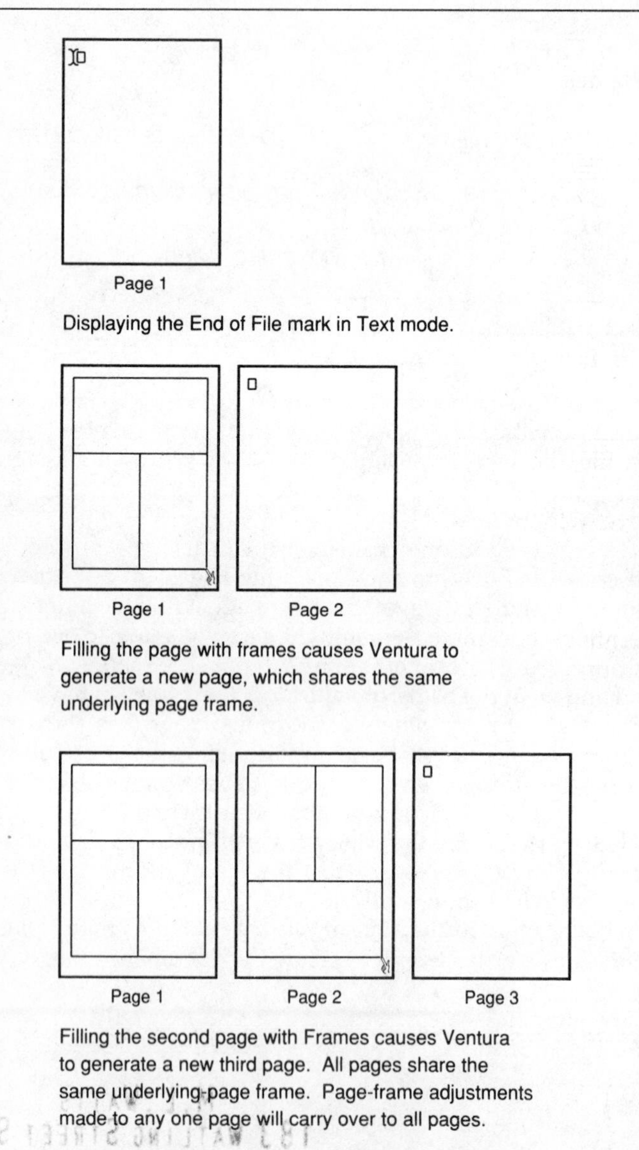

Figure 29: Filling a page with frames and generating additional pages automatically

SEE ALSO

Frames

Paragraph Mode, Paragraph Tags

See **Tags**.

Pictures

Ventura allows you to manipulate pictures (and the material around them) assigned to a frame (see **Text/Picture Files**) without affecting the original picture file.

VERSION

2.0, 1.1, 1.0

Cropping Pictures

SEQUENCE OF STEPS

To crop with the mouse:

Frame mode or also (2.0 only) **Graphics** mode *[point the mouse cursor anywhere on picture within*

the frame]
[press and hold Alt key]
[while holding Alt, drag the picture with the mouse]
[release the mouse button]

To crop by using offset settings (2.0 and 1.1 only):

Frame mode or also (2.0 only) **Graphics** mode
[click frame with picture]
Frame menu
Sizing & Scaling
[adjust X and Y Crop Offset settings]
OK or ↵

USAGE

Ventura provides two methods for cropping pictures. You can use the mouse or you can provide exact values to offset the picture from the frame.

In Frame mode or (2.0 only) Graphics mode, position the mouse cursor anywhere within the frame that holds the picture. Press the Alt key and, while holding it down, drag the picture with the mouse (press and hold the mouse button). When the picture is cropped as you like, release the mouse button. Before 2.0, you can use the mouse only if the scaled dimensions of the picture are greater than the dimensions of the frame that holds the picture. (See "Setting Scale Factors," below.)

To crop by providing exact values, use the Frame mode or (2.0 only) Graphics mode. Click the frame with the picture to select it. Then, use the Frame menu and choose **Sizing & Scaling**. In the dialog box, adjust the values for X Crop Offset and Y Crop Offset, along with the respective Plus (+) and Minus (–) buttons. Use X Crop Offset to adjust the picture left (+) and right (–) with respect to the frame. Use Y Crop Offset to adjust the picture up (+) and down (–).

With the frame selected, use the Frame menu's Sizing and Scaling dialog box and set X Crop Offset and Y Crop Offset to zero. (You can press the Esc key to delete the values, which sets them to zero.)

EXAMPLE

Assume that you have a picture, originally 3 inches high, that has the middle third showing in a frame that's 1 inch high. To show the top third of the picture in the frame, set the Y Crop Offset to 1 inch and click the Minus (–) button. Ventura will adjust the picture down the frame and display the top third (see Figure 30).

SEE ALSO

Frames

Hiding Pictures

SEQUENCE OF STEPS

To hide all pictures associated with a chapter:

[2.0 only: no picture frame selected]
Options menu
Hide All Pictures

(2.0 only) To hide one or more selected pictures:

Frame mode or also **Graphics** mode
[select the picture or pictures]
Options menu
Hide This Picture

Initial Position

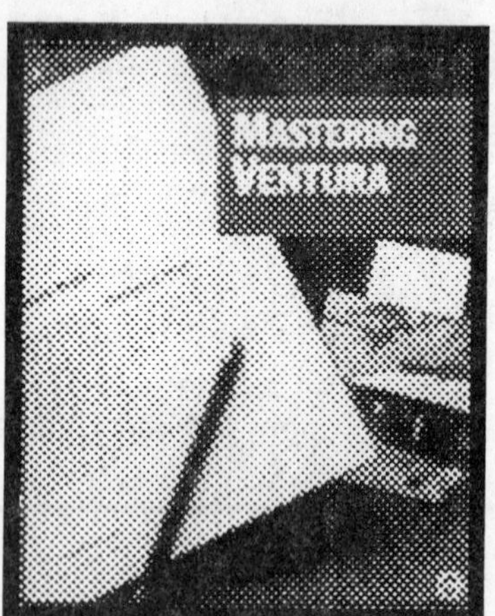

Minus (-) Y Crop Offset

Figure 30: Offsetting a picture down its frame

USAGE

Displaying pictures can slow Ventura's operations because it takes extra time both to redraw the screen and to print the document. Use these procedures to temporarily "hide" the pictures. Ventura replaces the pictures with a solid block.

You can hide all the pictures associated with a chapter when any of Ventura's four modes is activated. With version 2.0, if Ventura is in the Frame mode, you must not have any frame selected that has a picture assigned to it. Use the Options menu and choose Hide All Pictures.

With version 2.0 you can hide one or more selected picture frames. Other pictures will remain visible. In Frame mode, select the picture that you want to hide. To select multiple pictures, use the Shift key as you click. Then, use the Options menu and choose Hide This Picture. (This is the same option as for hiding all pictures, but the wording changes with a picture selected.) Ventura 2.0 stores the Hide/Show status of each picture frame with the chapter when you save.

UNDO

To display all hidden pictures, with no picture selected (2.0), use the Options menu and choose Show All Pictures. To display only one or more selected pictures, use the Frame mode and select the picture(s) you want to display. Then use the Options menu and choose Show This Picture.

SEE ALSO

Frames

Setting Scale Factors and Adjusting Aspect Ratio

SEQUENCE OF STEPS

Frame mode or also (2.0 only) **Graphics** mode
[select picture frame]
Frame menu
Sizing & Scaling
Picture Scaling: **Fit in Frame** or **By Scale Factors**
Aspect Ratio: **Maintained** or **Distorted**
[if Picture Scaling: By Scale Factors, *adjust* **Scale Width** *if desired]*
[if Picture Scaling: By Scale Factors *and* Aspect Ratio: Distorted, *also adjust* **Scale Height** *if desired]*
OK or ↵

USAGE

Use these procedures to adjust the size of a picture. In Frame mode, click the frame with the picture. Then, use the Frame menu and choose Sizing & Scaling. Adjust the settings according to the following guidelines. Then click **OK** or press ↵.

- *Picture Scaling: Fit In Frame.* Picture changes with the frame. As you change the size of the frame, Ventura will automatically adjust the size of the picture to fit inside.
- *Picture Scaling: By Scale Factors.* Ventura will allow you to adjust the size of the picture, independent of the size of the frame, by providing measurements (discussed below). Pictures smaller than the frame will have white space around them; pictures larger than the frame will be cropped.
- *Aspect Ratio: Maintained.* With pictures larger or smaller than the original, Ventura will maintain the picture's

aspect ratio. That is, the ratio of the picture's height to its width will remain the same so that the picture is not distorted.

- *Aspect Ratio: Distorted.* Ventura will adjust the dimensions of a picture in one direction or another as necessary, not attempting to keep the height-to-width ratio consistent. As a result, the picture may appear distorted.
- *Scale Width.* The width of the picture as scaled. You can adjust this setting only if Picture Scaling is set to By Scale Factors. For example, if you provide a value of 2 inches, Ventura will reduce or enlarge the picture as necessary to make it 2 inches wide. (With Picture Scaling: **Fit In Frame,** Ventura inserts the width of the frame into this field and scales the width of the picture to that value.)
- *Scale Height.* The height of the picture as scaled. You cannot enter a value into this field unless you've chosen the settings Picture Scaling: **By Scale Factors** and Aspect Ratio: **Distorted**. (With Picture Scaling: Fit In Frame, Ventura inserts the height of the frame and scales the height of the picture to that value. With Aspect Ratio: **Maintained,** Ventura calculates and inserts a value that will keep the aspect ratio, based on the value you provide for Scale Width.)

TIP

When using scanned images, for best results use the image in its original size or in evenly scaled factors. When you select Picture Scaling: **By Scale Factors**, Ventura will initially display the size of the picture. If necessary, use multiples of that value (half, double, triple, and so on) to scale the image. Failure to do so may result in moiré wavy patterns in your image. (Even so, you may see moiré patterns on the screen; you can ignore them because they won't appear when you print the document.)

SEE ALSO

Frames

Gray Scaling and Halftones

VERSION

2.0 only

SEQUENCE OF STEPS

Frame mode or also **Graphics** mode
[select frame with scanned image]
Frame menu
Image Settings
[adjust settings]
OK or ↵

USAGE

The Image Settings dialog box is for controlling the way Ventura creates halftones for pictures that meet the following specific criteria. To affect the printed version of the document, the picture must (1) be a scanned image, (2) be in PostScript or TIFF format, (3) contain gray scaling (the dots that make up the image must be shades of gray rather than simply black), and (4) be printed on a PostScript printer.

The halftone process converts the scanned image's gray dots to small black dots of varying density. Thus, the printer, which can print only black dots, seems to print shades of gray.

In Frame or Graphics mode, click the frame holding a scanned image that meets the criteria given above. Use the Frame menu to select Image Settings. Adjust the settings and give the OK.

In the Image Setting dialog box, you can set Halftone Screen Type to **Default**, **Dot**, **Line**, **Ellipse**, or **Custom**. Default is the usual setting. However, if Default produces an undesirable pattern in the printed image, or for a special effect, you can use one of the others. Normally, set Halftone Screen Angle to **45** (degrees). This rotates any undesired pattern, to make it less noticeable. Lines Per Inch relates the capabilities of your printer to Ventura. Set it to **60** for most laser printers, which are capable of 300 dpi (dots per inch). Set it to **90** for 1200 dpi typesetters and to **50** for 2540 dpi typesetters.

UNDO

With the frame selected, use the Frame menu's Image Settings. Change the settings to the usual ones given above.

Printing

Ventura allows you to print by sending its output to a printer, disk drive, or other device.

VERSION

2.0, 1.1, 1.0

Setting Printer Information

SEQUENCE OF STEPS

Options menu
Set Printer Info

[adjust settings]
OK or ↵

USAGE

Use the Set Printer Info dialog box to provide Ventura with preliminary print information. Ventura stores the settings when you quit, and they reappear the next time you use Ventura.

Use the Options menu and choose Set Printer Info. In the resulting dialog box, adjust the settings as discussed below. Then click **OK** or press ↵ to register your settings.

The first grouping in the Set Printer Info dialog box is for Device Name. The names of the printers you installed will appear on the buttons for Device name. If you installed only one printer, only that printer will appear and will always be selected. If you change the name of the printer you want to use, you will probably want to change the width table, too, as described below.

Use the Screen Fonts field to indicate the extension Ventura should use when loading fonts that appear on the screen. Use this field to add new screen fonts. Some examples are CGA for Color/Graphics Adapter, EGA for Enhanced Graphics Adapter, PSF for PostScript, VGA for full-page displays.

Use the Output To grouping to direct the output to one of the three parallel ports:

LPT1 LPT2 LPT3

two serial ports:

COM1 COM2

or two other destinations:

Direct Filename

Use Direct to send the output directly to devices that don't use ports, such as the JLaser card. Use Filename to "print" output files to disk, discussed next.

Printing Output Files Use the Filename button to direct the output to the disk. When you print to the disk, Ventura will provide an Item Selector box that you use to give a name to the output file, which normally has a C00 extension. The disk that you send the output to must have enough room to accommodate all the files associated with the document, as Ventura combines these documents into one large file.

Note that you can use the COPY command in DOS, without Ventura, to print or otherwise redirect the file.

Changing Width Tables The width table contains information that relates the fonts you have installed with the printer you are using. The style sheet records the name of the width table you use.

You must use a width table that matches the printer you are using to obtain the proper output for the printer. When you do, the word *Ultimate* appears at the top of the dialog box (or the bottom before version 2.0). You can use a width table—one that matches the printer you will ultimately use—with a different printer, to get an idea of how a document will ultimately look. The line endings will appear as they will on the final printer, but fonts and spacing between words and letters may be thrown off. The result is of Draft quality, which appears in place of Ultimate.

Click the command button labeled

Load Different Width Table (i.e. Font Metrics)

An Item Selector box appears that lists the width table files with the WID extension. Load the width table you want. Your selection is stored as part of the style sheet.

You can also use the OUTPUT.WID file. This width table is the same as that of the first printer listed in the Set Printer Info dialog box. By selecting this width table you can prepare a document for later printing on different equipment or with different fonts. The style sheet will automatically use the width table that matches the default printer.

UNDO

To restore the original settings, use Options menu/Set Printer Info and readjust the settings.

SEE ALSO

Fonts

Initiating Printing

SEQUENCE OF STEPS

File menu
To Print
[adjust settings or (2.0 only) leave them as is to print the currently displayed page]
OK or ↵

USAGE

Use this procedure to begin printing the displayed chapter. (To print publications, see **Publications**.)

Use the File menu and choose **To Print**. You'll see the Print Information dialog box. To print the currently displayed page (version 2.0), leave the settings and click **OK** or press ↵. (Before 2.0, Ventura prints that entire chapter as the default.)

The Print Information dialog box shows five settings for Which Pages:

All	The entire displayed document
Selected	The page numbers you provide in the fields below the setting
Left	Only the left-hand pages (1.1, 2.0)

Right	Only the right-hand pages (1.1, 2.0)
Current	Only the page currently displayed

Use the Left and Right buttons to create double-sided printouts on printers that use stacked paper. First use the Left button and print all the left-hand pages in the document. Then remove the stack of paper from the printer's output tray, flip the stack over, and print the right-hand pages with the Right button. You may need to add a final blank page before printing if the document ends on a right-hand page.

Use From Page and Through Page in conjunction with Which Pages: **Selected** to indicate the pages of the document you want Ventura to print. Ventura will use the page numbers that appear on the Side-bar. Use the Number Of Copies field to indicate how many copies you want to print.

If you're printing multiple copies, you may wish to set Collated Copies: **On**. Ventura will print entire copies of the document one by one. However, collating may take quite a bit longer to print than not collating, especially with pictures. When pages are not collated, Ventura can load all the pictures, fonts, and other settings into the printer for one page and print as many copies of the page as needed. When the pages are collated, Ventura must reload each time it prints the page.

Set Printing Order to **1st To Last** or **Last To 1st**, depending on the way you want the pages to land in your printer's output bin. Choose the setting your printer needs to create a properly ordered document. Set Paper Tray to **Default**, **Alt #1**, or **Alt #2** to indicate which of your printer's fresh paper trays (if more than one is available) you want Ventura to use. Use Paper Tray: **Manual** for envelopes that you insert one at a time with printers that pause for you to do so.

You can set Crop Marks: **On** to print crop marks that indicate the corners of the page when you use the Chapter menu's Page Size & Layout dialog box to indicate a page smaller than the actual paper you print on. Graphic designers and layout photographers use crop marks to position pages accurately.

In 2.0 only, set Spot Color Overlays: **On** to have Ventura print a different version of each page of the document, one for each color in the Paragraph menu/Define Colors dialog box set to Enabled. For further discussion of this ability, see **Colors**.

You can use the Multi-Chp Print Files setting only when you are printing a publication to a file. For more on using this ability, see **Publications**.

The Device Name and Output To fields (which, combined, are called Configuration before version 2.0) cannot be changed directly in this dialog box. They indicate the setup you have chosen with Options/Set Printer Info and can only be changed there.

Oversized Printing If you have used Chapter menu/ Page Size & Layout to specify a paper size larger than what Ventura suspects your printer can handle, Ventura will provide alternatives for you when you print. You'll see a dialog box and you can click one of the buttons:

Shrink: To reduce the page to fit (PostScript printers only).

Overlap: To print pages with some overlap so you can paste them together.

Nothing: To print full size.

If you choose Overlap, Ventura will provide you with alternative ways to overlap. Some methods will not work with all printers. For example, broadsheet printing in strips works only with typesetting machines.

SEE ALSO

Publications; Fonts

Publications

Use publication files to link chapters together.

VERSION

2.0, 1.1, 1.0

USAGE

A publication file is a listing of chapters (the publication list) that you want Ventura to consider as a unit. The elements are not combined on the disk and cannot be viewed in succession, but Ventura can perform a variety of operations on a publication. For example, it can carry over some elements, such as page numbering, from chapter to chapter (2.0 only).

Use the first procedure below to build a publication by inserting or adding chapters to it. Procedures that follow show how the resulting publication file can be saved and retrieved from the disk and printed and how its chapters can be moved within (reordered) or removed from the publication. You can also create an index to the publication (see **Index**), a table of contents for it (see **Table of Contents**), and copies of all files associated with the publication or a chapter from it—see "Opening (Retrieving) a Publication File" below.

The procedures use the Multi-Chapter Operations dialog box. To get to the Multi-Chapter Operations dialog box from Ventura's main screen, use the Options menu to click **Multi-Chapter**. (If you've been working on a chapter with unsaved changes, Ventura may ask you if you wish to save the current chapter.) The Multi-Chapter Operations dialog box displays the current chapter you've been working on or the last publication you worked with.

Adding Chapters to Build a Publication

SEQUENCE OF STEPS

Options menu **Multi-Chapter**
Add Chapter

[use Item Selector box to choose a chapter]
OK or ↵

USAGE

You can add a chapter to an existing publication or begin building a new publication by adding chapters to an empty publication list. To add a chapter to the current publication that appears in the Multi-Chapter Operations dialog box, click the chapter that you want the newly added chapter to appear after, which positions the darkened selector bar on that chapter. To clear the publication list so you can begin creating a new publication, click **New**.

Then click **Add Chapter.** Use the Item Selector box that appears to select the chapter you desire. The chapter will then appear on the publication list.

UNDO

Remove the chapter using the procedure described under "Removing a Chapter." Or, if you saved the publication before you added the chapter, you can click the **Done** box and then **Abandon**. To remove all chapters to start work on a new publication, click **New**.

Saving a Publication File

SEQUENCE OF STEPS

Options menu **Multi-Chapter**
Save or **Save As**
[use the Item Selector box to assign a name, if necessary]

USAGE

Use these procedures to save on disk the publication file you've been working on. In the Multi-Chapter Operations dialog box, with the publication displayed, click **Save** to save the publication file. If this is the first time for saving the publication, Ventura will display an Item Selector box so you can assign a name to the publication file. Or click **Save As** to save the publication file under another name and make a copy of it.

UNDO

Use the File menu's DOS File Operations dialog box to delete the unwanted publication file from the disk. To find the publication to remove, use the file specification *.PUB to filter for publication files only.

Opening (Retrieving) a Publication File

SEQUENCE OF STEPS

Options menu **Multi-Chapter**
[no file selected]
Open
[use the Item Selector box to select the desired PUB file]
OK or ↵

USAGE

You open a publication to retrieve a publication file from the disk. An opened publication file allows you to see the chapter files associated with it and to perform multi-chapter operations with it, such as indexing the publication, making a table of contents from it, copying all its associated files, and printing it.

In the Multi-Chapter Operations dialog box, first make sure no chapter file is selected. That is, no chapter listed should be darkened with a selection bar. (To deselect a chapter, click some spot in the dialog box other than a chapter's name.) Then click **Open**. Use the Item Selector box that appears to open the publication (PUB) file that you want. The chapter files that make up the publication will then appear on the publication list.

UNDO

In the Multi-Chapter Operations dialog box, use the **Open** procedure to open a different publication, or click **New** to empty the publication list and start work on a brand new publication.

Displaying a List of Files Associated with a Chapter

SEQUENCE OF STEPS

Options menu **Multi-Chapter**
[click a chapter file's name]
Open

USAGE

This procedure is similar to the previous one, which lists the chapters associated with a publication. Here, though, you list the files associated with a chapter. This procedure also shows the drives and directories that hold the files.

First, you must have the Multi-Chapter Operations dialog box displayed, showing the name of the chapter you want to examine. Click the file's name to select it. If the chapter's name does not appear, open the publication file that it is a part of to display it. Or, if the chapter is not a part of a publication but is loaded in the working area, click **New** and then **Done** to go back to the working area and use Options menu/Multi-Chapter again; the file's name will appear on the publication list, selected.

With the chapter name selected, click **Open**. The box will list the files associated with that chapter.

UNDO

When completed with your examination of these files, click **Close**. This will redisplay the publication list.

Moving a Chapter

SEQUENCE OF STEPS

Options menu **Multi-Chapter**
[in publication list, position the mouse cursor on the name of the chapter you want to move]
[press the mouse button and drag the chapter name to a new location]
[release the mouse]

USAGE

Use this procedure to move a chapter name to a different position on the publication list. Doing so rearranges the order of the chapters for printing and other procedures. You can have Ventura automatically renumber the chapters and other elements; see **Numbering Adjustments**.

Display the listing of chapters associated with the publication by opening or building the publication as described above. Then, position the mouse cursor on the name of the chapter you want to move. Drag the chapter to the new location by pressing and holding the mouse button as you move the mouse. The cursor changes into the shape of a flattened hand, and a ghosting bar moves with it to the new location. Release the mouse and the chapter name snaps to the new position.

TIP

Note that if the displayed list shows only a portion of the chapter names in the publication, you may not be able to re-position the chapter with one drag. Drag the chapter name as far down or up as possible. When you release, Ventura will scroll the publication list in the direction you are headed, relocating the chapter name and leaving it selected. You can then drag the chapter again to reach the location you want.

UNDO

Use the same procedure to move the chapter back to its original location. Or, if you saved the publication before you moved the chapter, click **Done** and then **Abandon** to retain the saved version.

Removing a Chapter

SEQUENCE OF STEPS

Options menu **Multi-Chapter**
[click a chapter file's name]
Remove Chap

USAGE

This procedure removes a chapter from a publication. The chapter remains on the disk, but it is no longer associated with the displayed publication. You can have Ventura automatically renumber the remaining chapters; see **Numbering Adjustments**.

With the listing of chapters associated with publication displayed, click the chapter you want to remove. Ventura darkens the file name to indicate it's selected. Then choose **Remove Chap**. The chapter's name disappears from the publication listing, and the files that follow it move up to fill in the gap.

UNDO

Since the removed file remains on the disk, simply use the Add Chapter procedure to reinsert the chapter into the publication.

Printing a Publication

SEQUENCE OF STEPS

Options menu **Multi-Chapter**
[publication listed, no file selected]
Print
[adjust setting in Print Information dialog box]
OK or ↵

USAGE

Use this procedure to print a publication. Ventura will print the chapters associated with the publication in the order listed. Ventura will handle numbering (such as page numbers) from chapter to chapter according to settings within the chapters; see **Numbering Adjustments**.

Start with the Multi-Chapter Operations dialog box displaying the publication you want to print. (Use **Open** to open the publication if necessary.) Then click **Print**. The Print Information dialog box will appear, just as it does when you print a chapter (see **Printing**). Adjust the settings as you do when printing a chapter. Then click **OK** or press ↵.

TIP

Multi-Chp Print Files will usually ghost in the Print Information dialog box, as it does when you print a chapter. It is available only when printing a publication and when you've used Options menu/Set Printer Info to specify Output To: **Filename** (see **Printing**). Use it to combine all output chapters you're "printing" to disk into one file or to direct each to a separate file. Once you start to "print," Ventura will request a name for the output file. For separate file output, Ventura will add the extensions C00, C01, C02, and so on to each file in succession.

If you place all your front matter into one chapter file, Ventura will assign it to the C00 file. Then, your Chapter 1 would become the C01 file, your Chapter 2 would become the C02 file, and so on.

UNDO

To interrupt printing, press the Esc key. Ventura will finish printing the page it is working on and cancel the rest of the print job.

SEE ALSO

Printing

Copying a Publication or Chapter

SEQUENCE OF STEPS

Options menu **Multi-Chapter**
[select chapter or provide publication name if necessary]
Copy All
[provide destination directories]
OK

USAGE

Use this procedure to copy a publication or chapter, along with all the files associated with it, including its style sheets, width tables, text files, and picture files.

When copying a chapter's files, only the chapter file whose name has been selected (darkened) will be copied. If necessary, select **New** and then **Add Chapter** to load a chapter file to copy. Once you load the chapter's name onto the list, click the name to select it for copying.

To open a publication for copying, make sure no chapter file is selected and choose **Open**. To copy the entire publication, no chapter name should be selected. (To deselect a chapter, click some spot in the dialog box other than a chapter's name.)

When copying the chosen chapter or publication, choose **Copy All**. In the dialog box that appears, you'll see an indicator giving the name of the publication or chapter you designated. Provide a destination directory for each of the file categories listed (publications and chapters, style sheets and width tables, and so on). To send all files to the same directory, provide the first destination (for PUB & CHP files), and then click the command button labeled

Make All Directories The Same As The First.

and click **OK**.

Note that you must click the **OK** button to initiate the copying process. You cannot use the ↵.

UNDO

Use File menu/DOS File Operations to remove copies from the disk. If you copy all related files to one directory, it's easy to remove them all in case of an error. Set the drive and directory path, plus wildcards (*.*) and remove all the files in that directory.

SEE ALSO

Chapters

Quitting

Use this procedure to end a work session with Ventura.

VERSION

2.0, 1.1, 1.0

SEQUENCE OF STEPS

File menu
Quit
(if prompted for verification) **Save** or **Abandon**

USAGE

Use the File menu and click **Quit**. If you've made changes (edits) to the displayed chapter since you last saved, Ventura will display the message:

STOP
Save or Abandon changes
to this chapter?

Select one of the three buttons presented: **Save**, to save your edits and then quit Ventura; **Abandon**, to quit Ventura without saving your edits. You can also use **Don't Quit**, which keeps Ventura operational, but changes are not yet saved. Then, you can use File menu/Save (or Ctrl-S to save).

When you quit, Ventura stores several of its operational settings; these settings are the same when you next run the program. The settings Ventura stores include the final operating mode (Frame, Paragraph, Text, or Graphics), the final view (Reduced, Normal, Enlarged, or Facing Pages), and most of the Options settings (see **Options**).

Its always wise to use Quit when you are finished so Ventura can properly store these settings on the disk. Don't just turn the computer off. Ventura stores settings in files with the INF extension, usually in the VENTURA directory (see Appendix A). To regain Ventura's original settings, delete these files.

TIP

Even though the Save button is designed to save before quitting, don't rely on it to do so. If the disk is full, Ventura will not save for you when quitting, and you can lose your work. Always use File menu/Save (or Ctrl-S) to save before you quit.

UNDO

Load Ventura again by typing **VP** at the operating system prompt. Files abandoned when quitting cannot be regained.

Removing

Removing (cutting) text, frames, graphics, see **Cut/Copy/Paste**.
Removing a chapter from a publication, see **Publications**.
Removing files from disk, see **DOS File Operations**.
Removing files from frames, see **Text/Picture Files**.
Removing tags, see **Tags**.

Reverse Type (and Related Effects)

You can use several methods to create reverse type (white on black) and related effects, including frames, box text, and paragraph tags.

VERSION

2.0, 1.1, 1.0

Reverse Type with Frames

SEQUENCE OF STEPS

Frame mode or also (2.0 only) **Graphics** mode
[click or create a frame]
Frame menu
Frame Background

Color: **Black**
Pattern: **Solid**
OK or ↵

USAGE

Use this procedure to create reverse type within a frame. With it, you change the frame's background to black. Black text within the frame automatically changes to white.

Activate the Frame mode (or also Graphics mode in 2.0) and click the frame you desire. Then use the Frame menu and choose Frame Background. In the resulting menu, select Color: **Black** and Pattern: **Solid**. Click **OK** or press ↵.

You can use a similar procedure to change the Pattern or Color of the background. (See **Graphics** for samples of the patterns.) Black fonts will not change to white with other patterns or colors; however, you can change the font color of paragraphs that you use (see **Fonts**).

These procedures work with standard frames or with the underlying-page frame.

UNDO

Use the same procedure and reset the frame background. Default settings are Color: **Black**, Pattern: **Hollow.**

EXAMPLE

See Figure 31.

SEE ALSO

Frames

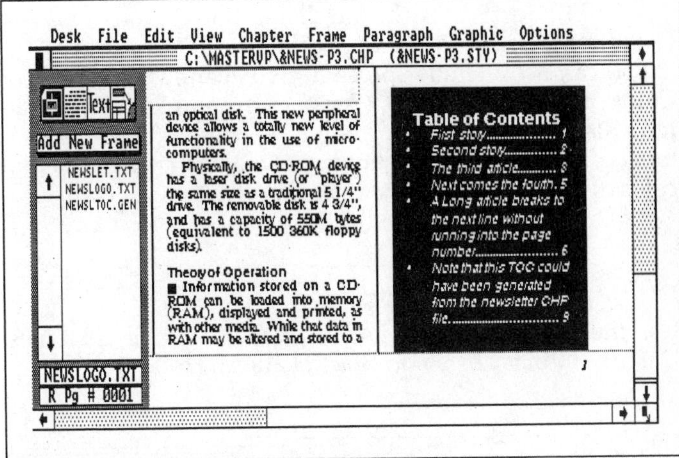

Figure 31: Reverse type within a frame

Reverse Type with Box Text

SEQUENCE OF STEPS

Graphics mode
[click or create Box Text box]
Ctrl-F or **Graphic** menu/**Fill Attributes**
Color: **Black**
Pattern: **Solid**
OK or ↵

USAGE

Use this procedure to create reverse type with box text. With it, you change the box's fill attributes to black. Black box text within the box automatically changes to white.

Use the Graphics mode and click or create the box (see **Graphics**). Then type **Ctrl-F** or use the Graphic menu to choose **Fill Attributes**. In the dialog box that appears, set Color to **Black** and Pattern to **Solid**. Click **OK** or press ↵.

You can use a similar procedure to change the Pattern or Color of the fill attributes. (For pattern samples, see **Graphics**.) Black fonts will not change to white with other pattern/color combinations; however, you can change the font color of paragraphs that you use if necessary (see **Fonts**).

UNDO

Use the same procedure and reset the box's fill attributes. Default settings are Color: **Black,** Pattern: **Hollow.**

SEE ALSO

Graphics

Reverse Type with Paragraphs

SEQUENCE OF STEPS

Paragraph mode
[select a paragraph]
Paragraph menu/**Font**
Color: **White** *[note font size]*
OK or ↵
Paragraph menu/**Ruling Line Above**
[set **Width***]*
Color: **Black**; Pattern: **Solid**
Height Of Rule 1: *[provide value equal to the noted font size or larger]*
Space Below Rule 3: *[provide value slightly larger than (point size of font plus Height of Rule 1) divided by 2]*

Minus (–) button
OK or ↵

USAGE

Use this procedure to create reverse type that's associated with a paragraph tag. You do this by changing the font to white. Then you create a wide black ruling line above the paragraph and lower the line behind the text. All paragraphs similarly tagged will receive the same effect. The procedure will work only for paragraphs that contain no more than one line of text.

Using the Paragraph mode, select a paragraph with text you want to appear in reverse type. Then, in the Paragraph menu/Font dialog box, select Color:**White**. Note the font size in the dialog box and give the OK. Because of the White setting, the text will seem to disappear.

Then, use Paragraph menu/Ruling Line Above. Set **Width** for the setting you desire for the darkened bar (see **Line Drawing**). Select Color: **Black** and Pattern: **Solid**. For Height of Rule 1, specify a value equal to the font size you noted or larger. For Space Below Rule 3, provide a value you determine as follows: add the point size of the font to the value you've specified for Height Of Rule 1, divide the result by 2, and then insert a value that is slightly more than this amount. Click the **Minus (–)** button to lower the rule. Then click **OK** or press ↵.

You can vary the settings for Color and Pattern. By doing so, you can create shaded type or other effects.

TIP

Once you have this effect set up, you may find that it disappears when you are in the process of editing the text. Press the Esc key to "re-ink" the screen, and you will see the text, properly displayed white against black.

UNDO

Use Paragraph/Font and change Color to **Black.** Then, using Paragraph menu/Ruling Line Above, set Width to **None.**

SEE ALSO

Tags

Rotating Text

You can rotate text in increments of 90 degrees.

VERSION

2.0 only

SEQUENCE OF STEPS

Paragraph mode
[click a paragraph]
Paragraph menu
Alignment
Text Rotation: **90** or **180** or **270**
Maximum Rotated Height: *[provide a value]*
OK or ↵

USAGE

Use this procedure to change the orientation of the text for paragraphs with a given tag. Some printers, such as the LaserJet, will not be able to print more than one orientation on the page.

Activate the Paragraph mode and click a paragraph to adjust the rotation of its tag. Use the Paragraph menu and choose **Alignment**. In the Alignment dialog box, set Text Rotation to **90**, **180**, or **270**, depending on the degree of rotation you want. Then provide a value for Maximum Rotated Height. Ventura uses this value for the height of the area in which it rotates the text. (The width is the normal width that would be available even if the text was not rotated.) Click **OK** or press ↵.

TIP

When you edit, use the cursor keys as you would if the text were not rotated. Thus, with 90 degree rotation, to move the text cursor up and down the text as it appears on the screen, you use the → and ← keys, respectively. If text is rotated 180 degrees (upside down), you move the cursor left with the → key, right with the ← key.

UNDO

With a paragraph selected, use Paragraph menu/**Alignment** and set Text Rotation: **None**.

EXAMPLE

See Figure 32.

SEE ALSO

Text

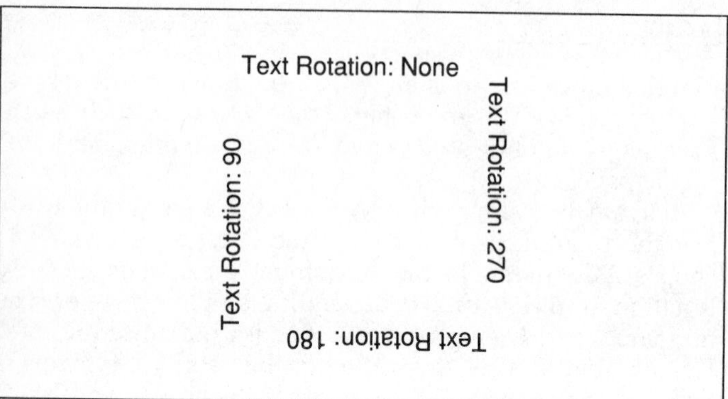

Figure 32: Text rotation

Rulers

You can have Ventura display rulers for use in placing text, frames, and graphics on the screen.

VERSION

2.0, 1.1, 1.0 (Adjusting rulers not available for version 1.0.)

Displaying Rulers

SEQUENCE OF STEPS

Options menu
Show Rulers

USAGE

If rulers are not appearing at the top and left of the working area, you can use this procedure to display them. On the Options menu, select **Show Rulers**, and the rulers will appear. Then, as you move the mouse cursor on the screen, corresponding hairlines that indicate its position move along the rulers. (Hairlines do not appear in version 1.0.)

When Ventura represents the mouse cursor with bracketed symbols (such as the bracketed FR for adding a new frame), the ruler hairlines correspond to the bracket's corner (top-left of the symbol). With pointing symbols (such as the arrow in the Graphics mode), the hairlines correspond to the tip of the pointer. For other symbols, the hairlines correspond to the center of the symbol.

UNDO

To remove rulers that appear alongside the working area, use the Options menu and choose **Hide Rulers**.

EXAMPLE

See Figure 33.

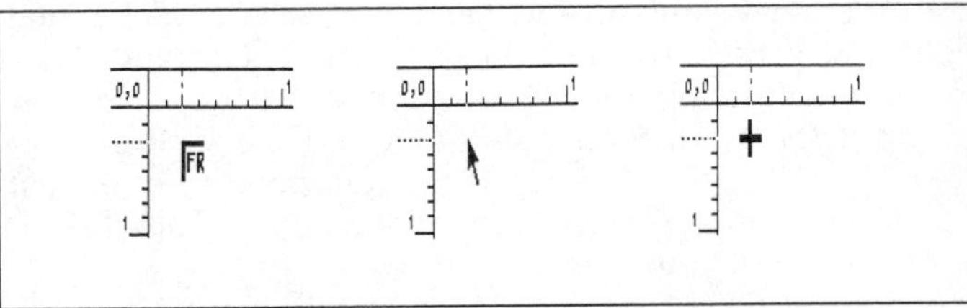

Figure 33: Ruler hairlines indicating the position of the mouse cursor

Adjusting Rulers

SEQUENCE OF STEPS

To indicate the units of measurement and adjust the zero point by providing values:

Options menu
Set Ruler
[adjust settings]
OK or ↵

To adjust the zero point with the mouse:

[point to the 0,0 box]
[drag mouse to the desired location]
[release the mouse]

USAGE

You can stipulate the units of measurement Ventura should use for the rulers. You can also reposition the zero point by providing values or by using the mouse.

To indicate the units of measurement to use, use the Options menu and choose **Set Ruler.** In the Set Ruler dialog box, you'll see that you can independently set the Horizontal Units and Vertical Units for Inches, Centimeters, and Picas. Select the setting you desire. You can also use this dialog box to adjust the Horizontal Zero Point and the Vertical Zero Point. Providing a value offsets the zero point from the left (Horizontal) or top (Vertical) by that amount. Click **OK** or press ↵ to effect your choices.

You can also use the mouse to relocate the zero point. Position the mouse cursor on the 0,0 box at the top left, where the rulers meet. Then drag the mouse to the position you desire. As you do, the mouse cursor changes to a four-headed arrow and cross hairs appear, intersecting at the mouse cursor.

Release the mouse button and Ventura relocates the zero point and the cross hairs disappear.

TIP

If you release when the mouse cursor is in the working area, Ventura relocates the zero point of both rulers. If you release when the mouse cursor is pointing to only one ruler, Ventura relocates only the zero point of that ruler.

You can use cross hairs to check alignment of elements appearing on the page—such as frames, graphics, or the edges of text—even if you don't want to change the zero point. Do so by not releasing the mouse until you position it back at the 0,0 box. Alternatively, reset the zero point in the normal location by using one of the undo procedures below.

UNDO

Click the 0,0 box at the top left of the working area or use the Options menu/Set Ruler dialog box to set the Horizontal and Vertical Zero Point to zero.

EXAMPLE

See Figure 34.

Ruling Lines

See **Line Drawing.**

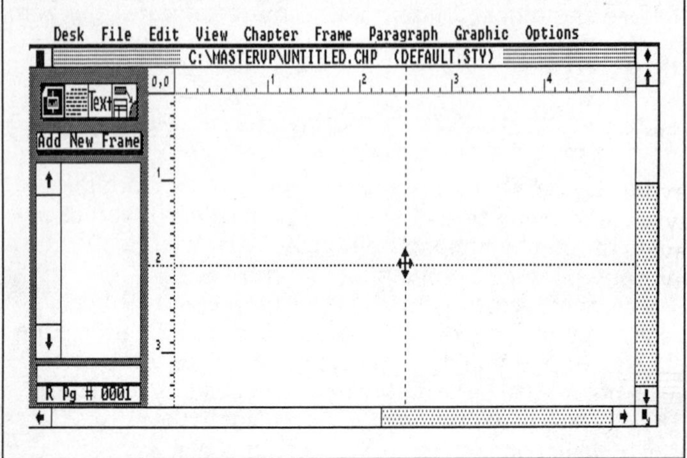

Figure 34: Cross hairs

Saving

Saving chapters, see **Chapters**. (Saving a chapter also saves revised elements of the chapter, such as its text files.)
Saving publications, see **Publications**.
Saving style sheets, see **Style Sheets**.

Side-bar

See Appendix B: Elements of Ventura Screens.

Spacing

Ventura provides various ways to control spacing for paragraphs and lines, frames, and between words and letters.

VERSION

2.0, 1.1, 1.0 (Typographical spacing not available with 1.0)

Vertical Paragraph and Line Spacing

SEQUENCE OF STEPS

Paragraph mode
[select a paragraph]
Paragraph menu
Spacing
Above, Below, Inter-Line, Inter-paragraph: *[provide values]*
Add In Above: **Always** or **When Not At Column Top**
OK or ↵

USAGE

Use these settings to control the vertical spacing for a tag. Paragraphs with the same tag receive the same treatment.

Activate the Paragraph mode and click a paragraph whose tag you wish to adjust. Use the Paragraph menu and choose **Spacing**. Use the top four fields as follows to adjust the vertical spacing of paragraphs and lines of text: **Above** guarantees the amount of space above paragraphs with the tag, and **Below** guarantees the amount of space below with the tag. **Inter-Line** sets the distance from the top edge of one line of text to that of the next line, and **Inter-Paragraph** sets the amount of spacing added between paragraphs with the same tag, or between differently tagged paragraphs when the value is *identical* for both paragraphs. Click **OK** or press ↵ to effect your choices.

In the same dialog box, use Add In Above: **When Not At Column Top** to make Ventura remove spacing above a paragraph (set with the Above field) whenever the paragraph appears at the top of a column or page. Use Add In Above: **Always** and Ventura will always insert the Above space before the paragraph.

TIP

If you increase the size of a font for text within a paragraph (see **Fonts**), with version 2.0 you can have Ventura automatically increase the spacing between the line that the larger font appears in and the line above it. With earlier versions, the large font could overlap the text on the line above it. To accomplish this, activate the Paragraph mode and click the paragraph. Use Paragraph menu/Paragraph Typography to set Grow Inter-Line To Fit: **On.** With this setting Off, Ventura keeps the inter-line spacing the same, even if a larger font appears on a given line.

UNDO

Use the same procedure to readjust the spacing. Some believe that single spacing should be two points greater than the font size (check Paragraph menu/Font); others prefer a setting of 1.2 times greater than the font size. For 10-point fonts, either rule of thumb suggests 12 points for single spacing.

EXAMPLE

See Figure 35.

SEE ALSO

Fonts; Tags

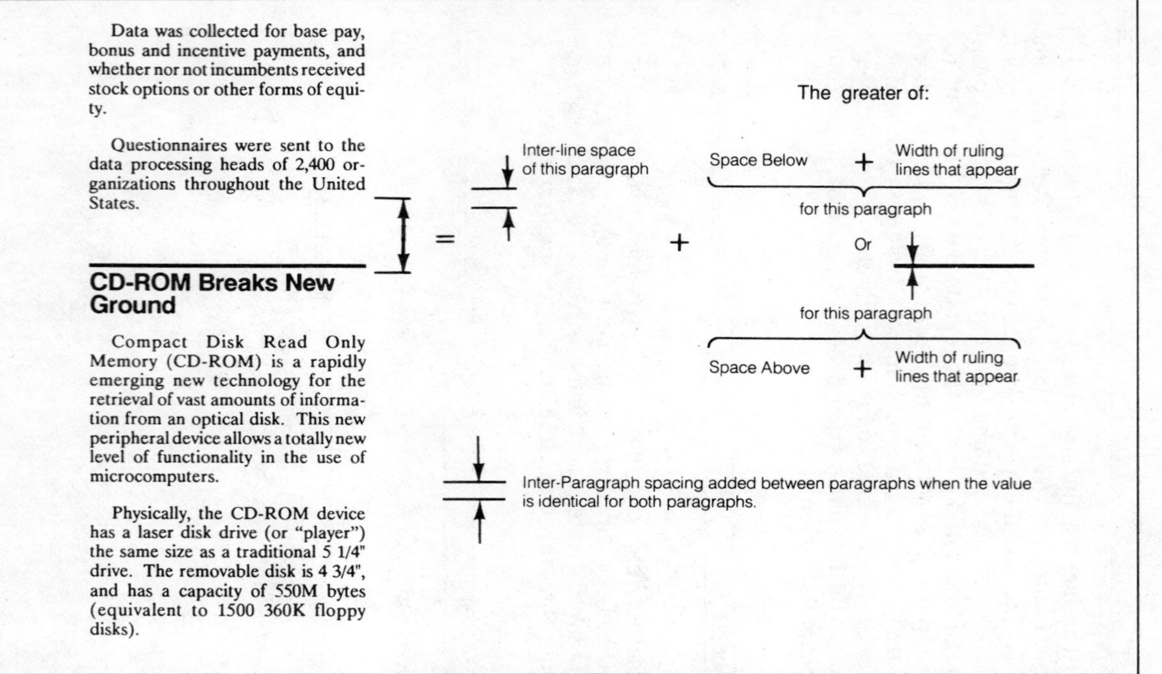

Figure 35: How Ventura determines the space between paragraphs

Set-in Paragraphs (Temporary Margins)

SEQUENCE OF STEPS

Paragraph mode
[select a paragraph]
Paragraph menu
Spacing
Settings For: **Left Page** or **Right Page**
In From Left or In From Right: *[provide values]*
[Click Inserts: **Copy To Facing Page** *if desired]*
OK or ↵

USAGE

Use this procedure to set selected paragraphs further in from the margins of the page or column in which they appear. It adds a "temporary" additional margin, temporarily decreasing the column width set for the frame with Frame menu/ Margins & Columns. The set-in value may be in addition to other values that will provide additional spacing to **offset** the text even more (see Figure 36).

Activate the Paragraph mode and click the paragraph whose tag you wish to adjust. Use the Paragraph menu and choose **Spacing**. In the Spacing dialog box,

Settings For: Left Page Right Page

will indicate the current-sided page, along with its settings for In From Left and In From Right. (The Settings For buttons affect only the In From Left and In From Right values; they have no effect on the paragraph and line space settings, described above, that appear in the same dialog box.) Provide these fields with measurements to set in paragraphs that share the same tag. For double-sided documents (set with Chapter menu/Page Size & Layout), you can then click the

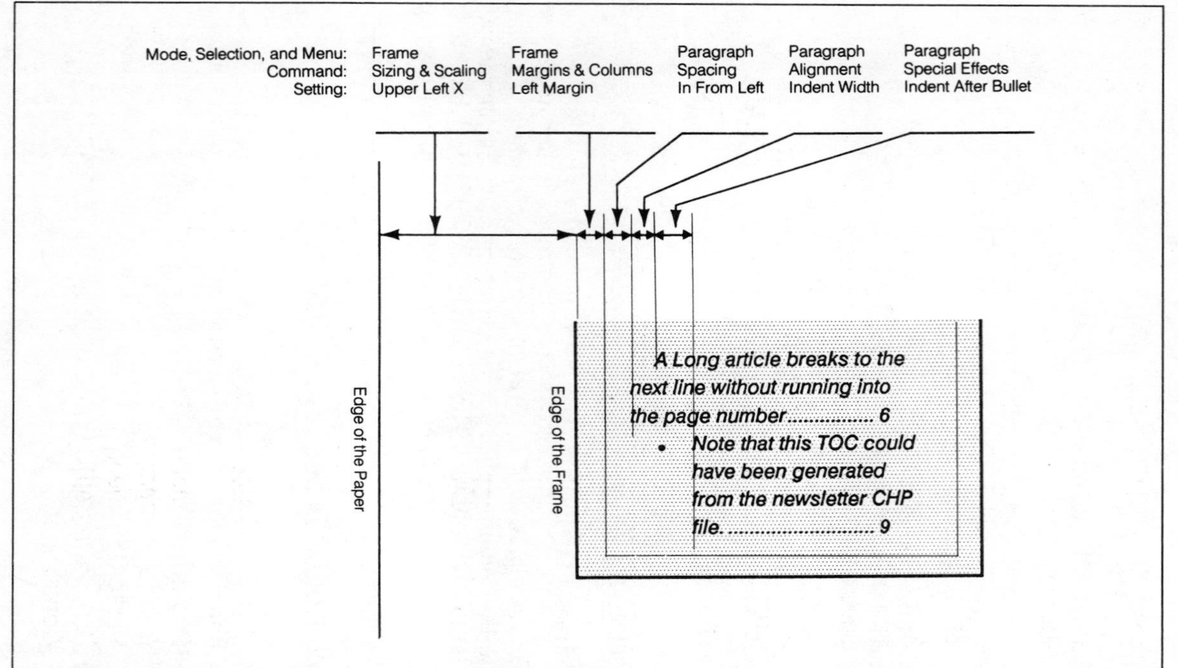

Figure 36: Horizontal spacing settings

opposite Settings For button and provide values for opposite pages. Alternatively, click Inserts: **Copy To Facing Page** and Ventura will exactly copy (not mirror) your values to the opposite page. Click **OK** or press ↵ to effect your settings.

UNDO

With the paragraph selected, use Paragraph menu/Spacing and set In From Left and In From Right to zero. (You can simply use the Esc key to wipe out the values.)

EXAMPLE

See Figure 36.

SEE ALSO

Frames, Margins, Tags

Spacing Between Words and Letters

VERSION

2.0 and 1.1 only.

SEQUENCE OF STEPS

Paragraph mode
[click a paragraph]
Paragraph menu
(2.0) **Paragraph Typography**; (1.1) **Typographic Controls**

[adjust settings for Letter Spacing or Tracking]
OK or ↵

USAGE

Use these settings to control the spacing between words and letters in a selected paragraph and in all similarly tagged paragraphs. Letter spacing regulates space added between letters to achieve justification in each line. Tracking regulates spacing between letters added to entire paragraphs. (These features are not available in version 1.0).

Activate the Paragraph mode and click a sample paragraph whose tag you want to adjust. Then use the Paragraph menu and choose **Paragraph Typography** (or, in version 1.1, **Typographic Controls**). Adjust the appropriate settings as described below and click **OK** or press ↵.

Letter spacing applies only to justified text. It determines whether Ventura justifies by adding space between letters and words or between words only. In the dialog box, the settings that regulate letter spacing are

Letter Spacing: On *[or]* Off   Up To: 0.100 Ems

With Letter Spacing: **On**, Ventura justifies text by adding space between letters and words. With Letter Spacing: **Off**, it justifies by adding space between words only. Use the Up To field to indicate an amount in ems up to which Ventura can add spacing between letters. Theoretically, an em space is equal in width to the capital letter M in the font you're using. (In version 2.0, Ventura uses the @ symbol.) Up To: **0.100** Ems is the standard setting. Figure 37 shows the result of various adjustments to these settings.

Tracking controls spacing between all letters and words, expanding or shrinking it uniformly for all similarly tagged paragraphs. It operates whether the text is justified or not. In the dialog box, the settings that regulate tracking are

Tracking: Looser *[or]* Tighter   0.000 Ems

Use tracking to increase or decrease the room that text occupies (Figure 38) or to match line lengths (Figure 39). Provide a value in ems to make the text looser or tighter (as you select) by that amount.

Acme Magazine asked Joe Smith, a compensation consulting specialist for the software industry, to design and conduct the survey. Twenty-four positions, representing four programmer job families plus management, were included.

Letter Spacing Off

Acme Magazine asked Joe Smith, a compensation consulting specialist for the software industry, to design and conduct the survey. Twenty-four positions, representing four programmer job families plus management, were included.

Letter Spacing On, Up to .05 Ems

Acme Magazine asked Joe Smith, a compensation consulting specialist for the software industry, to design and conduct the survey. Twenty-four positions, representing four programmer job families plus management, were included.

Letter Spacing On, Up To .1 Ems

Figure 37: Various letter spacing treatments

Acme Magazine asked Joe Smith, a compensation consulting specialist for the software industry, to design and conduct the survey. Twenty-four positions, representing four programmer job families plus management, were included.

Tracking 0

Acme Magazine asked Joe Smith, a compensation consulting specialist for the software industry, to design and conduct the survey. Twenty-four positions, representing four programmer job families plus management, were included.

Tracking .01 Ems Tighter

Acme Magazine asked Joe Smith, a compensation consulting specialist for the software industry, to design and conduct the survey. Twenty-four positions, representing four programmer job families plus management, were included.

Tracking .01 Ems Looser

Figure 38: Various tracking treatments

History
of the
Universe

Figure 39: Using tracking to match line lengths

The three Space Width fields—Minimum, Normal, and Maximum—apply to spacing between words. Ventura multiplies the value you supply by the normal width of a space (as contained in the width table) and displays the result in ems. For example, if you enter **2** and the width of a space is .25 ems, Ventura will display:

2.000 * (space width) = 0.500 Ems

assigning a value of 1/2 em to the Space Width field you are using.

Normally, spacing between words is the same amount as that of the standard width of a space. Thus, the value specified for Normal Space Width is usually 1. With justified text, Ventura will use the value you specify as the average. As necessary, Ventura will decrease the space between words, but no less than the amount you indicate for Minimum Space Width. Ventura does not use Maximum Space Width to restrict the amount of space it will allow, but will flag as loose lines wherever it must exceed this value. (Use Options menu/**Show Loose Lines** to see them.)

UNDO

With a paragraph selected, use Paragraph menu/Paragraph Typography. For no letter spacing, set Letter Spacing: **Off**. For no tracking, delete the Letter Spacing value for ems. Adjust the Space Width values; some typical settings are Minimum: .6; Normal: 1, and Maximum: 2.

EXAMPLE

See Figure 40.

SEE ALSO

Kerning

Solid (Fixed) Spaces

SEQUENCE OF STEPS

Enter special space characters with Ventura or your word processor as shown in Table 3.

Acme Magazine asked Joe Smith, a compensation consulting specialist for the software industry, to design and conduct the survey. Twenty-four positions, representing four programmer job families plus management, were included.

Normal Space Width: 1

Acme Magazine asked Joe Smith, a compensation consulting specialist for the software industry, to design and conduct the survey. Twenty-four positions, representing four programmer job families plus management, were included.

Normal Space Width: .8

Acme Magazine asked Joe Smith, a compensation consulting specialist for the software industry, to design and conduct the survey. Twenty-four positions, representing four programmer job families plus management, were included.

Normal Space Width: .6

Figure 40: Changing the normal space width setting

<table>
<tr><th>TYPE OF SPACE</th><th>DESCRIPTION</th><th>VENTURA</th><th>WORD PROCESSOR</th></tr>
<tr><td>Em</td><td>Width of letter M (width of @ in 2.0)</td><td>Ctrl-Shift-M</td><td><_></td></tr>
<tr><td>En</td><td>Half an Em space</td><td>Ctrl-Shift-N</td><td><~l></td></tr>
<tr><td>Figure (1.1 and 2.0 only)</td><td>Width of a numeral</td><td>Ctrl-Shift-F</td><td><+></td></tr>
<tr><td>Thin</td><td>Width of a period</td><td>Ctrl-Shift-T</td><td><|></td></tr>
<tr><td>NoBreak</td><td>Keeps text together</td><td>Ctrl-Space</td><td><N></td></tr>
</table>

Table 3: Space characters in Ventura

USAGE

Use these special codes to create solid (fixed) space characters. These space characters are always the same size for the particular font you're using. They do not expand and shrink to accommodate justification as standard spaces (created with the space bar) do.

Use either the listed Ctrl-key code in Ventura or the code with your word processor. Ventura also supports some word processors' own means of creating the NoBreak Space. For example, in Microsoft Word use Ctrl-Space; in WordPerfect, use Home, Space.

UNDO

In Ventura, use the Delete key or the Backspace key to delete a special space character, just as you would any character (see **Text**). Or use your word processor's deleting capabilities (generally the Delete and Backspace keys as well).

SEE ALSO

Text

Special Effects

See **Big First Characters, Bullets.**

Strike-thru

See **Underline/Overscore/Strike-thru**.

Style Sheets

Use style sheets to store the attributes of tags and the underlying-page frame.

VERSION

2.0, 1.1, 1.0 (Printing the style sheet available with version 2.0 only.)

USAGE

A style sheet is a compilation of settings for various layout and other formatting attributes, as well as a collection of paragraph tags and each of their format settings. Each chapter has one style sheet associated with it, which the chapter references to set these features. However, more than one chapter can reference the same style sheet. Table 4 shows the menu items that control the style sheet.

Ventura saves changes that you make to a style sheet when you save the chapter. When you load Ventura or use File menu/New to start work on a new chapter, Ventura loads the last style sheet you used.

MENU	SELECTION
File	Load Diff Style Save as New Style
2.0: Chapter; 1.0, 1.1: Page	2.0: Page Size & Layout; 1.0, 1.1: Page Layout Auto-Numbering
Frame (Underlying-Page frame only)	Margins & Columns Sizing & Scaling Vertical Rules Ruling Line/Box Frame Background
Paragraph	All
Options	Set Printer Info (Width Table setting only)

Table 4: Menu choices that affect style sheets

Loading a Style Sheet

SEQUENCE OF STEPS

File menu
Load Diff Style
[use Item Selector box to select a style sheet file]
OK or ↵

USAGE

Use this procedure to associate a different style sheet with the chapter you're working on. The style sheet settings will apply to the chapter, and its list of tags will become available for applying to paragraphs in the chapter.

Use the File menu and choose **Load Diff Style**. An Item Selector box will appear; use it to load the style sheet you wish applied to the chapter. Then click **OK** or press ↵. The chapter will use the new style sheet, as indicated by the appearance of the style sheet name on the Title Bar. Ventura will record the name of the style sheet when you save the chapter. When you load the chapter again, Ventura will load the same style sheet.

TIP

When you load a different style sheet, Ventura may find that your chapter has tag names that are not contained on the style sheet. In that case, Ventura will add the tag names to those already on the style sheet, displaying them on the Assignment list in all capital letters, and provide them with the attributes of the Body Text tag.

UNDO

Using the File menu, click **Load Diff Style**. Load the original style sheet.

SEE ALSO

Tags

New Style Sheet

SEQUENCE OF STEPS

File menu
Save As New Style
[change directories if desired]
[provide a new file name]
OK or ↵

USAGE

Use this procedure to provide a new name for a style sheet. Ventura will make a copy of the style sheet, saving it on disk under the new name.

Use the File menu and click **Save As New Style**. In the Item Selector box that appears, you can change directories by clicking the backup button at the top left of the item selector list. You can also move the text cursor to the Directory field and edit the indicated path.

Provide a new name for the style sheet. Normally, you do not need to add the standard STY extension as part of the file name. Ventura will automatically add STY to names given without an extension as long as it appears as part of the Directory field, such as

Directory: C:\SYBEX*.STY

Click **OK** or press ↵. The chapter will reference the new style sheet, whose name will appear on the Title Bar. Ventura will save the association when you save the chapter.

UNDO

Using the File menu, click **Load Diff Style**. Load the style sheet under the old name. Use File menu/DOS File Ops to delete the newly created style sheet.

Printing a Style Sheet

SEQUENCE OF STEPS

(Version 2.0 only) To create a text file that lists tags and settings for the style sheet:

Paragraph mode
Ctrl-K or **Paragraph** menu/**Update Tag List**

[If asked whether to save or abandon changes:] **Save**
Command: **Print Style Sheet**
[assign a name to the generated text file]
OK or ↵

Then, to print the text, you must assign it to a new chapter, using the generated STYLOG.STY style sheet, and print.

USAGE

Printing a style sheet with Ventura requires two main operations. First, you use a special procedure to create a generated text file that lists tags and settings for the style sheet. Then you use standard Ventura procedures to create and print a document that uses this text file as it would one created with a word processor.

Activate the Paragraph mode. Then press Ctrl-K or use Paragraph menu/Update Tag List. (If you've been working on a chapter and have unsaved changes, Ventura will ask you if you want to save your work.) Use the Update Tag List dialog box and click **Print Style Sheet**. An Item Selector box will appear; use it to assign a name to the text file. Normally, you do not need to add the standard GEN extension as part of the file name. Ventura will automatically add GEN to names given without an extension as long as it appears as part of the Directory field, such as

Directory: C:\SYBEX*.GEN

Click **OK** or press ↵ and Ventura will generate the file.

Next use File menu/New to clear the screen so you can compile your style sheet document. Then use File menu/Load Diff Style to load a special style sheet, provided with Ventura, that's geared to the listing. It's in the TYPESET directory and it's the STYLOG.STY file. Then, in Frame mode, click the underlying-page frame and use File menu/Load Text/Picture to load the text file. Specify Text Format: **Generated** and use the Item Selector box to load the file. Then, print the document as usual (see **Printing**).

UNDO

You can use File menu/DOS File Ops to delete the generated text file from the disk (see **DOS File Operations**).

Subscript/Superscript

Ventura can create subscript text—text shifted below standard text on the same line—and superscript text—text shifted above standard text.

VERSION

2.0, 1.1, 1.0

Shifting Selected Text

To shift text by using the Assignment list:

Text mode
[select the text]
Assignment list: **Superscript** or **Subscript**

To shift by using the Set Font button:

Text mode
[select the text]
Side-bar: **Set Font** button
Shift: **Up** or **Down**
[provide value for amount of shift]
OK or ↵

USAGE

These two procedures allow you to subscript and superscript text by assigning it as a text attribute. Using the Assignment list is quicker, but using the Set Font button gives you more control over the individually selected text.

To use the Assignment list, activate the Text mode and select the text by dragging the mouse across it or using Shift-click (see **Text**). Then, on the Side-bar's Assignment list, select **Superscript** or **Subscript**. Ventura will insert Attribute Setting codes at the beginning and end of the selected text that raise or lower the text as you've indicated.

To use the Set Font button, use Text mode to select the text. Then click the **Set Font** button. In the Set Font dialog box, use Shift: **Up** to create superscript text; use Shift: **Down** to create subscript text. Next, provide a value for the amount (distance) of shift you desire. Click **OK** or press ↵.

UNDO

On the selected text, use the Assignments list's Normal assignment to unshift the text. Or use the Delete key to remove the Attr Setting codes at the beginning and end of the shifted text. See **Fonts** for more on undoing text attributes.

Adjusting Subscript/Superscript Attributes

VERSION

2.0 only

SEQUENCE OF STEPS

Paragraph mode
[click a paragraph]

Paragraph menu
Attribute Overrides
[for Superscript or Subscript, adjust **Size** *and* **Shift By** *values]*
OK or ↵

USAGE

These settings control shift attributes by the tag. They affect text you shift by using the Assignment list's Superscript or Subscript assignments. The attributes you specify apply to the selected paragraph as well as all paragraphs with the same tag.

In Paragraph mode, click a paragraph. Then use the Paragraph menu and choose Attribute Overrides. In the dialog box that appears, you'll see fields for

Superscript Size:	Shift ↑ By:
Subscript Size:	Shift ↓ By:

Provide values in the Size field to set the point size of the font Ventura uses for subscript and superscript text. Provide a value for the Shift By fields and Ventura will use the values you provide to shift the text up or down by that amount. Then click **OK** or press ↵.

UNDO

With the paragraph selected, use Paragraph menu/Attribute Overrides again. Reset the original values. Typical values for 12-point type are Size: 10, Shift ↑ By: 05.64 fractional points; Shift ↓ By: 01.32 fractional points.

Shifting Up and Down with Your Word Processor

SEQUENCE OF STEPS

To indicate superscript, as if assigned with the Assignment list:

<^>*[text to superscript]***<D>**

To indicate subscript, as if assigned with the Assignment list:

<V>*[text to subscript]***<D>**

To indicate shift ("jump") up or down, as if set with the Set Font button:

<J*[amount of shift]***>***[text to shift]***<J0>**

USAGE

Insert these codes into word processor text to indicate superscript or subscript as if assigned with Ventura's Assignment list. Alternatively, you may be able to use your word processor's procedures for superscript and subscript. You can also indicate shift up or down as if set with the Set Font button.

To indicate superscript as if assigned with the Assignment list, enter a left angle-bracket (<), followed by a caret (^), and a right angle-bracket (>). Then enter the text you wish to superscript. To end superscript, enter the **<D>** code. Superscript also ends with a paragraph return or with another code.

To indicate subscript as if assigned with the Assignment list, enter a left angle-bracket (<), followed by the letter V, and a right angle-bracket (>). Then enter the text you wish to subscript. To end subscript, enter the **<D>** code. Subscript also ends with a paragraph return or with another code.

If Ventura supports your word processor's superscript and subscript capabilities, you can use them instead. The effect is the same as if you had used the two procedures just described.

For example, with Microsoft Word, you create superscript with Alt-Plus, subscript with Alt-Minus. With WordPerfect, superscript with Ctrl-F8, 1, 2; subscript with Ctrl-F8, 1, 1.

You can also use a "jump" code to indicate a shift up or down and specify the amount of the shift with a jump value as well. The effect is the same as if you had used Ventura's Set Font button to shift text. Enter a left angle-bracket (<), followed by the letter J, and a jump value (described below) from 1 to 255. Then enter a right angle-bracket (>) and the text you wish to superscript. To end shifting, enter the **<J0>** code. Shifting also ends with a paragraph return or with another code.

To determine the jump value, first decide the amount, in points, you wish to shift the text up or down. Then, to shift the text down, multiply that value by 4.166 and round it. To shift up, also multiply by 4.166 but subtract the result, rounded, from 256.

UNDO

Use your word processor's delete capabilities to remove the codes from the text. You can also use Ventura's procedures, described above, to delete the text attribute codes.

EXAMPLE

To create $E=mc^2$:

E=mc<^>2<D>

To create H_2O:

H<V>2<D>O

Table of Contents

Ventura can automatically compile a table of contents using paragraph tags in your document.

VERSION

2.0, 1.1, 1.0

SEQUENCE OF STEPS

Options menu
Multi-Chapter
*[click **Save**, or press ↵, if requested]*
[open or save as a publication]
Make TOC
[adjust settings]
OK

USAGE

Use this procedure to generate a table of contents (TOC), which is a publication feature (see **Publications**). Use the Options menu and choose **Multi-Chapter**. If you have unsaved changes, Ventura asks whether you wish to save; click **Save** or press ↵. Then open the publication for which you wish to generate the TOC. (If you want a TOC for only one chapter file, you must save the chapter as a publication first.)

With the publication selected, click **Make TOC**. In the Generate Table Of Contents dialog box, you will see the default settings Ventura uses to generate the TOC. Once you've adjusted the settings as you desire, click **OK** to generate the

TOC. You must click the OK button to initiate the process; you cannot use ↵.

In the Generate TOC dialog box you can change the suggestions Ventura provides. TOC File is the name and directory location Ventura suggests for text file it will generate. It uses the first five characters in the name of the publication file and adds TOC (for table of contents) and the GEN extension (for generated).

Title String is the name Ventura will place at the top of the TOC file; normally the title string is simply the words *Table of Contents*. This text will automatically receive the generated tag Z_TOC TITLE.

Use the remaining field lines to indicate what tags Ventura should use to compile the TOC. You must recall the appropriate tag names; you cannot see a list of them at this point. Once the TOC generation begins, Ventura will search for text, such as chapter headings and section headings, having the tags you indicated. It will copy that text to create the TOC file, to which it will assign the tags Z_TOC LVL 1 for Level 1, Z_TOC LVL 2 for Level 2, and so on, in the TOC file. (These tags are already set up and formatted in the &TCHD-P1.STY sample style sheet.)

Use the Inserts buttons to insert special codes in the field lines. Click **Tab** to insert a Tab character (indicated by →). Click **Chapter #** to insert the [C#] code; when Ventura compiles the TOC, it will substitute the chapter number as set by Chapter menu/Update Counters in place of this code. (You can also simply type in the code yourself.) To understand how such numbering works within the chapter, see **Numbering Adjustments** and **Numbering Sections**. Click **Page #** to insert the [P#] code, which Ventura will replace with the appropriate page number. By clicking **Text Attr**, you insert the <D> code. Either click this button and replace the D with the appropriate text code or simply type in the entire bracketed code yourself. Codes are the same as those you would use to create a text attribute with a word processor (see Appendix C).

UNDO

If there is a problem with a generated table of contents, simply make your corrections and generate a new version of the TOC. Ventura will ask if you want to overwrite the previous version. You cannot retrieve the overwritten version.

SEE ALSO

Numbering (Counter) Adjustments; Numbering Sections; Publications; Tags; Text/Picture Files

Tables

You can create tables either by setting tab stops and using the tab character or by creating separate paragraph tags for each column in the table. (You can also create tables with Box Text; see **Graphics**.)

VERSION

2.0, 1.1, 1.0

Setting Tabs

SEQUENCE OF STEPS

Paragraph mode
[click a paragraph]
Paragraph menu

Tab Settings
[adjust settings for each Tab Number]
OK or ↵

USAGE

Use this procedure to set the tab stops for each paragraph bearing a given tag. Activate the Paragraph mode and click a sample paragraph whose tag you want to adjust. Then use the Paragraph menu and choose Tab Settings. In the resulting dialog box, you'll see the tab settings for the first of up to 16 tab stops, as indicated by

Tab Number: ← 1 →

in version 2.0 (previous versions indicate the tab number by a selected button). Use the ← and → buttons to change the tab number. As you do, the next three settings in the box will change to display the settings for each tab number in turn. Change them as you wish and, when you are finished, click **OK** or press ↵.

The first adjustment you can make for each Tab Number is Tab Type. Settings for Tab Type include Off, Left, Center, Right, and Decimal. If a Tab Number's Tab Type is set to Off, the settings below it will have no effect. The other settings determine the alignment of text that follows the Tab character (which is created by pressing the Tab key). Ventura positions the alignment with respect to the tab stop. With decimal tabs, the text is aligned with the decimal point. You can change the character Ventura uses as the decimal point with the Options menu's Set Preferences dialog box. In the Decimal Tab Character field, provide the character's ASCII value (see Appendix C).

You can set Tab Shown As to **Open Space** or **Leader Char**. Tab Shown As: **Open Space** will display nothing in the tab area (that is, the area covered by the Tab character leading up to the tab stop). Tab Shown As: **Leader Char** causes Ventura to use the leader character that you indicate in the field below to fill in the tab area. Use the field for Tab Location to specify the position of the tab stop, from the left edge of the paragraph.

The next three settings apply to all tab stops in the paragraph. Leader Char sets the default leader character. It affects all tab stops in the paragraph that are set for Tab Shown As: Leader Char. You can set Leader Char to one of four settings to fill the tab area as indicated:

Spaces

...

___

Custom

Choosing Spaces pads the tab area with blank spaces. (The effect is the same as choosing Tab Shown As: **Open Space.**) Choosing Custom allows you fill the tab area with any character by providing its ASCII value (see Appendix C) in the field right after Custom.

Leader Spacing dictates the number of spaces Ventura inserts between each leader character. The wider the distance spacing between tab stops, the more spacing between leader characters is desirable.

Auto-Leader is new with version 2.0. It causes the leader character you've specified, spaced as you've indicated, to appear after the Paragraph return that ends the paragraph. The leader characters fill in the area from the paragraph return to the right edge of the paragraph.

Column Tags

SEQUENCE OF STEPS

Paragraph mode
[select paragraph for first column]
Side-bar: **Add New Tag** button
[provide a name for the column 1 tag]
OK or ↵ (for the Add New Tag dialog box)

Paragraph menu
Spacing
[provide In From Left and In From Right values]
OK or ↵ (for the Spacing dialog box)
Paragraph menu
Breaks
[adjust Line Break and other settings]
OK or ↵ (for the Breaks dialog box)
[repeat for other columns]

USAGE

Use this technique to create different tags for each column in a table.

In Paragraph mode, select a paragraph for column 1. Click the Side-bar's **Add New Tag** button. Provide a name for the column 1 tag, such as Col 1, and click **OK** or press ↵.

Then use the Paragraph menu and choose Spacing. Set the In From Left value. This is the distance, usually 0 for column 1, from the left edge of the table to the left edge of the column (determined by the frame's margins). Provide the In From Right value, which is the distance from the right edge of the table to the right edge of the column. Then give the OK.

With the same paragraph still selected, use Paragraph menu/Breaks. Set Line Break to Before (see Figure 41), which will cause the text in that paragraph to begin on a new line. Set Allow Within to No, so that a break in text does not occur within the paragraph. Set Keep With Next to Yes so that Col 1 stays with Col 2. Give the OK.

Repeat the procedure, creating tags and adjusting their settings as the figure shows. Then apply the tags to each paragraph as appropriate.

TIP

If, when adding text, you want to start a new line but stay in the same column, do not use the ↵ key because the resulting

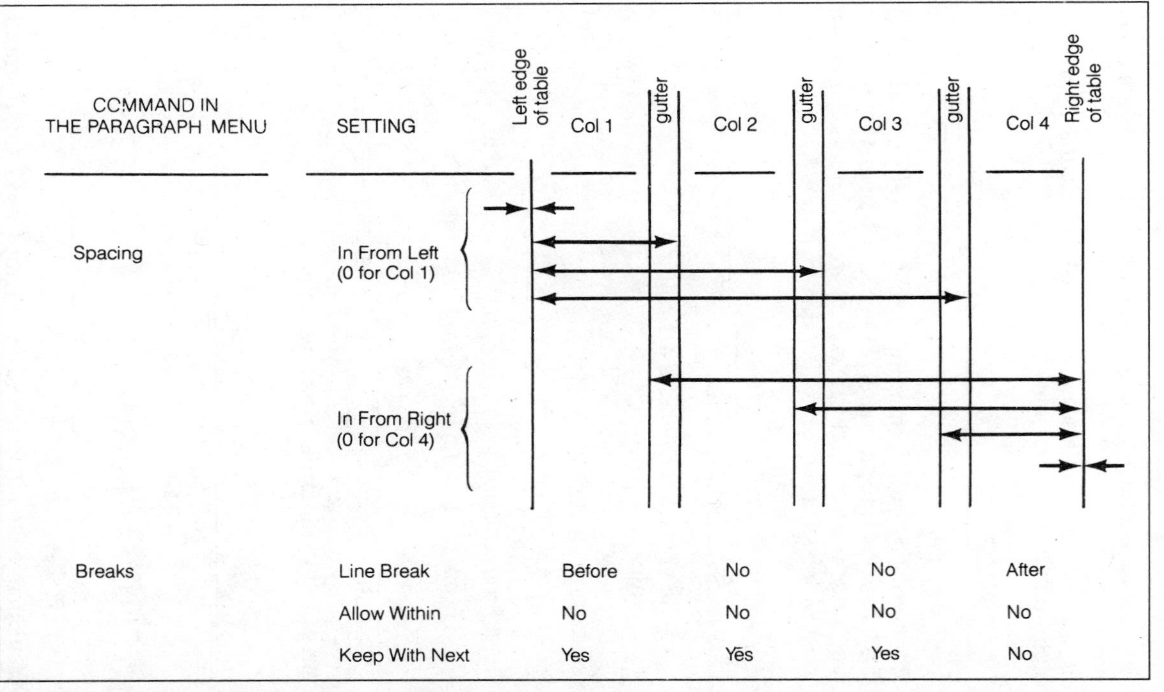

Figure 41: Settings that affect column tags

paragraph would begin in the same spot as the previous paragraph. Instead use **Ctrl-↵**, which creates a line break but keeps the same paragraph. Thus the text remains in the same column but starts on a new line.

UNDO

To remove column formatting from a tag, select a paragraph and use Paragraph menu/Spacing. Change the In From Left and In From Right fields to zero. Then use Paragraph menu/Breaks and set Line Break to Before & After.

EXAMPLE

Assume you want to create a 4-column table that's 5-1/2 inches wide. To make each column 1 inch with 3 gutters of 1/2 inch between each column, you'd use the following values:

Column:	1	2	3	4
In From Left:	0	1.5 in.	3 in.	4.5 in.
In From Right:	4.5 in.	3 in.	1.5 in.	0 in.

SEE ALSO

Breaking Paragraphs; Spacing; Tags

Tags

You change the attributes of a paragraph by changing the attributes of the paragraph's tag, or by changing tags.

VERSION

2.0, 1.1, 1.0

USAGE

Tags store attribute settings that you can repeatedly apply to chunks of text called paragraphs. Ventura determines the end of a paragraph (and hence the beginning of a new one) with a return. By applying the same tag to more than one paragraph, you cause each paragraph to receive the same attributes. Changes you make to the tag are then made to each paragraph so tagged.

Tags are stored in the style sheet. Each chapter that uses the same style sheet has the same set of tags, each tag with its own set of paragraph attributes.

Tagging procedures use the Paragraph mode. In the Paragraph mode, the Assignment list displays the names of tags that the style sheet has available. You can use the Paragraph mode to perform a variety of procedures, as described below, in building or altering this collection of tags. You can apply tags to paragraphs, add new tags to the list, rename tags, and remove them from the list.

You can also apply tags to paragraphs by using your word processor. However, you must use Ventura to assign attributes to the tags.

Body Text

Every style sheet has a default tag called Body Text. Usually, this tag is for the most common paragraph style in the document. You cannot remove this tag from the style sheet, and you cannot assign it a different name. Text you create with a word processor receives the Body Text tag, unless you assign a different tag as described below.

Ventura takes some cues for standard procedures from the Body Text tag. For example, if you use the Options menu to turn Line Snap on, frames you create will snap to the lines of text established by the Body Text tag (see **Options**).

Generated Tags

Ventura will automatically create and name tags as you perform certain procedures. These are called *generated* tags. Table 5 lists Ventura's generated tags, along with the applications for which it creates them. You can perform the same procedures on generated tags that you do on standard tags.

GENERATED TAG	FORMAT
Z_BOXTEXT	Box text
Z_CAPTION	Free form captions (Text mode)
Z_FNOT #	Footnote numbers: reference numbers (or symbols such as *) at the bottom of the page
Z_FNOT ENTRY	Footnote entries: text at the bottom of the page
Z_FOOTER	Footers
Z_HEADER	Headers
Z_LABEL CAP	Caption labels without an automatic number
Z_LABEL TBL	Caption labels with a table number
Z_LABEL FIG	Caption labels with a figure number
Beginning with Z_SEC	Automatic section numbers
Beginning with Z_INDEX	Entries in the index
Beginning with Z_TOC	Entries in the table of contents

Table 5: Generated tags

Normally, the names of generated tags do not appear on the Paragraph mode's Assignment list. However, you can make Ventura display them by using Options menu/Set Preferences and setting Generated Tags: **Shown.** Only those generated tags that Ventura has already created for the displayed chapter will appear on the Assignment list.

Activating Paragraph Mode

SEQUENCE OF STEPS

Paragraph button (at the top of the Side-bar)

or

View menu
Paragraph Tagging

or

Ctrl-I

USAGE

You activate the Paragraph mode to perform an operation on a tag. You can use any of three methods: click the **Paragraph** button, which is the second of four buttons at the top of the Side-bar; use the View menu and choose **Paragraph Tagging**; or press **Ctrl-I** on the keyboard.

UNDO

Use one of the methods for switching Ventura to one of its other modes (Frame, Text or Graphics mode).

EXAMPLE

See Figure 42.

SEE ALSO

Frames; Text; Graphics

Adding New Tags

SEQUENCE OF STEPS

Paragraph mode
[click a paragraph if desired]
Side-bar: **Add New Tag** button
Tag Name To Add: *[provide a new tag name]*
Tag Name To Copy From: *[change if desired]*
OK or ↵
[adjust attributes of the new tag as desired]

USING THE SIDE-BAR	USING THE VIEW MENU	USING THE KEYBOARD	RESULTING MOUSE SHAPE
	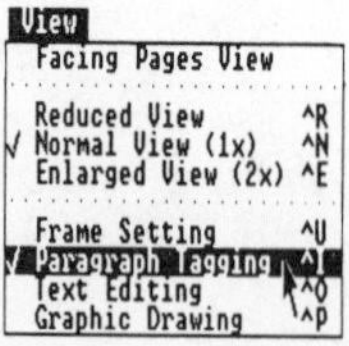 View Facing Pages View Reduced View ^R √ Normal View (1x) ^N Enlarged View (2x) ^E Frame Setting ^U √ Paragraph Tagging ^I Text Editing ^O Graphic Drawing ^P	 CTRL - I	

Figure 42: Activating paragraph mode

USAGE

Use this procedure to create a new tag and add it to the Paragraph mode's Assignment list. Once you've created a new tag, you can adjust its attributes and apply it to paragraphs. Ventura adds the new tag to the style sheet.

Activate the Paragraph mode and, optionally, click a paragraph for which you want to create the new tag or a paragraph with a tag whose attributes you want to use as a foundation for the new tag. Then, on the Side-bar, click the **Add New Tag** button.

In the dialog box that appears, for the Tag Name To Add field, make up a name for the new tag. In the Tag Name To Copy From field, Ventura will display the tag name of the paragraph you selected. (If you selected no paragraph, the name *Body Text* appears.) Change this field, if you wish, to use the attributes of another tag as a starting point for the new tag. Then click **OK** or press ↵. Ventura adds the new tag name to the Assignment list and assigns the new tag to the selected paragraph. You can then use the Paragraph menu to change the attributes of the tag, and you can select other paragraphs to which to assign the new tag.

TIP

Tag names on the Assignment list appear in alphabetical order, so to keep similar tags together, assign them names that have similar beginnings. For example, to keep three column tags together, you might name them Column #1, Column #2, and Column #3, rather than First Column, Second Column, and Third Column.

UNDO

To remove a newly created tag, see "Removing Tags," below.

Applying Tags in Ventura

SEQUENCE OF STEPS

Paragraph mode
[click a paragraph]
Assignment list: *[click tag name]*

To select multiple paragraphs for applying the tag to:

Shift-click the paragraphs

before using the Assignment list.

To assign tags to the Function keys:

(2.0) **Text** mode	(1.1, 1.0) **Paragraph** mode or Text mode
Ctrl-K	**Ctrl-K** or **Paragraph** menu/ **Assign Func Keys**
[make assignments]	*[make assignments]*
OK or ↵	**OK** or ↵

or

Paragraph mode
Ctrl-K or
Paragraph menu/**Update Tag List**
Save or ↵ if prompted
Assign Func Keys
[make assignments]
OK or ↵

USAGE

Ventura provides two ways for you to apply a tag to a paragraph. You can apply the tag directly to one or several paragraphs by using the Paragraph mode's Assignment list. Or you can assign the tag to one of the Function keys and use that key to apply the tag.

Applying the Tags Directly Select the Paragraph mode. Then, click the paragraph you want to apply the tag to. The paragraph's current tag assignment appears in the Current box. On the Assignment list, click the name of the tag you want to apply. The newly assigned tag name appears in the Current box, and the paragraph takes on the tag's attributes.

You can also apply the same tag to several paragraphs at the same time, as long as they appear on the same page. Click one paragraph, then hold down the Shift key as you click the others. The word *MULTIPLE* appears in the Current box. To deselect a paragraph if necessary, Shift-click it again. With the desired paragraphs selected, click the tag name.

Assigning Tags to the Function Keys Use either Paragraph mode or Text mode and press **Ctrl-K**. In the Text mode, this reveals the Assign Function Keys dialog box; provide tag names in the appropriate Function key fields and then click **OK** or press ↵. In the Paragraph mode of version 2.0, Ventura may first ask if you want to save changes to the chapter. Then it will present the Update Tag List dialog box. Click the **Assign Func Keys** button and Ventura displays the Assign Function Keys dialog box, which you can use as you do in the Text mode.

In the Paragraph mode, instead of Ctrl-K, you can also use the Paragraph menu. From that menu, select **Update Tag List** (2.0) or **Assign Func Keys** (1.1 and 1.0).

Once you assign a tag to a Function key, you can apply the tag either in the Paragraph mode or the Text mode. In Paragraph mode, Ventura assigns the tag to the selected paragraph(s). In the Text mode, Ventura assigns the tag to the paragraph with the text cursor or the paragraph(s) with selected text.

UNDO

To change a paragraph's tag back to its original assignment, use the same procedures to reassign it.

Renaming Tags

SEQUENCE OF STEPS

Version 2.0:

Paragraph mode
[click a paragraph with tag to rename]
Ctrl-K or **Paragraph** menu/**Update Tag List**
Save or ↵ if prompted
Rename Tag
New Tag Name: *[provide new name]*
OK or ↵ for Rename Tag dialog box
OK or ↵ for Update Tag List dialog box
Save or **Save As** (↵) for Style Sheet

Version 1.1 and 1.0:

Paragraph mode
[click a paragraph with tag to rename]
Paragraph menu
Rename Tag
New Tag Name: *[provide new name]*
OK or ↵

USAGE

Use this procedure to rename a tag as it appears on the style sheet. Version 2.0 allows you to save the style sheet easily, rather than having to use the File menu as you must with earlier versions.

With 2.0, activate the Paragraph mode and click a paragraph that bears the tag you want to rename. Press **Ctrl-K** or use Paragraph menu/Update Tag List. Ventura may first ask if you want to save changes to the chapter. Then it will present the Update Tag List dialog box, with the name of the tag selected. Click the **Rename Tag** button. The Rename Tag dialog box appears, with the Old Tag Name field showing the tag you want to rename. In the New Tag Name field, make up a new name for the tag. Click **OK** or press ↵, and Ventura will display the Update Tag List dialog box again. Click **OK** or press ↵ again, and Ventura will ask if you want to save the tags' style sheet or save the tags as a new style sheet.

With version 1.1 and 1.0, use the Paragraph mode to select a paragraph with the tag you want to rename. Then use Paragraph menu/Rename Tag to display the Rename Tag dialog box and use it as described with version 2.0.

UNDO

With the paragraph that has the new tag name selected, use the same procedure to display the Rename Tag dialog box. Old Tag Name will show the newly assigned name. Use New Tag Name to reassign the original name.

SEE ALSO

Style Sheets

Removing Tags

SEQUENCE OF STEPS

Version 2.0:

> **Paragraph** mode
> *[click a paragraph with tag to rename]*

Ctrl-K or **Paragraph** menu/**Update Tag List**
Save or ↵ if prompted
Remove Selected Tag button
Tag Name To Convert To: *[indicate tag to apply to paragraphs]*
OK or ↵ for Remove Tag dialog box
OK or ↵ for Update Tag List dialog box
Save or **Save As** (↵) for Style Sheet

Version 1.1 and 1.0:

Paragraph mode
[click a paragraph with tag to rename]
Paragraph menu
Remove Tag
Tag Name To Convert To: *[indicate tag to apply to paragraphs]*
OK or ↵

USAGE

Use this procedure to remove a tag from the style sheet. Version 2.0 allows you to save the style sheet easily, rather than having to use the File menu, as you must with earlier versions.

With version 2.0, activate the Paragraph mode and click a paragraph that bears the tag you want to remove. Press **Ctrl-K** or use Paragraph menu/Update Tag List. Ventura may first ask if you want to save changes to the chapter. Then it will present the Update Tag List dialog box, with the name of the tag selected. (If you decide that you want to remove another tag, select it at this point.) Click the **Remove Selected Tag** button. The Remove Tag dialog box appears, with the Tag Name To Remove field showing the tag you want to rename. (This provides a second opportunity for you to remove another tag by entering its name instead.) In the Tag Name To Convert To field, provide the name of an existing tag that you want Ventura to apply to the paragraphs it removes the tag from. Click

OK or press ↵, and Ventura will display the Update Tag List dialog box again. Click **OK** or press ↵ again, and Ventura will ask if you want to save the tags' style sheet or save the tags as a new style sheet.

With version 1.1 and 1.0, use the Paragraph mode to select a paragraph with the tag you wish to remove. Then use Paragraph menu/Remove Tag to display the Remove Tag dialog box and use it as described with version 2.0.

UNDO

Ventura provides no method to directly regain a removed tag and its attributes once you've saved the style sheet. However, if you have used Option menu/Set Preferences to set Keep Backup Files: Yes and saved the style sheet prior to removing the tag, you can retrieve the backup style sheet with the STY extension (see **Style Sheets**).

SEE ALSO

Style Sheets

Assigning Tags with Your Word Processor

SEQUENCE OF STEPS

@tag name = text of paragraph

USAGE

Use the syntax above to tag a paragraph in a text file with your word processor. This method of assigning tags is sometimes called preformatting. When you load the file into Ventura (see **Text/Picture Files**), Ventura automatically applies the tags to the paragraphs, and the paragraphs take on the attributes that you've assigned to the tags. If Ventura finds a tag name in the text file that does not exist in the style sheet, it adds the tag to the Assignment list in all capital letters, giving it the attributes of the Body Text tag.

At the beginning of the paragraph, type the At symbol (@) followed by the name of the tag you want to apply, a space, the Equal sign (=), another space, and then text of the paragraph. You must place the @ symbol at the very beginning of the paragraph. The tag applied ends with the Paragraph End code, created by pressing ↵. You do not need to assign the tag with Body Text paragraphs; for any paragraphs that you don't provide with a tag, Ventura assigns the Body Text tag.

SEE ALSO

Text

Text

You activate the Text mode to edit the text of the document and to set text attributes.

VERSION

2.0, 1.1, 1.0

Activating Text Mode

SEQUENCE OF STEPS

Text button (at the top of the Side-bar)

or

View menu
Text Editing

or

Ctrl-O

USAGE

You can use any one of three methods to activate the Text mode: click the **Text** button; use the View menu and choose **Text Editing**; or press **Ctrl-O**.

UNDO

Use one of the methods for switching Ventura to one of its other modes (Frame, Paragraph, or Graphics mode).

EXAMPLE

See Figure 43.

SEE ALSO

Frames; Graphics; Tags

USING THE SIDE-BAR	USING THE VIEW MENU	USING THE KEYBOARD	RESULTING MOUSE SHAPE
 Text	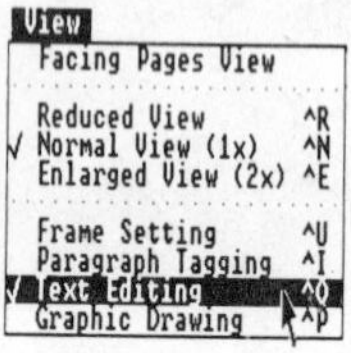 View Facing Pages View Reduced View ^R √ Normal View (1x) ^N Enlarged View (2x) ^E Frame Setting ^U Paragraph Tagging ^I √ Text Editing ^O Graphic Drawing ^P	 CTRL - O	 I

Figure 43: Activating Text mode

Editing Text

SEQUENCE OF STEPS

To insert the text cursor into the text on the page:

Text mode
[position the mouse on the spot in the text]
[click the mouse]

To move the text cursor from one spot to another on the page:

↑ or ↓ or ← or →

To insert text at the text cursor:

[type the text]

To delete the character at (to the right of) the text cursor:

Delete key

To erase the character before (to the left of) the text cursor:

Backspace key

USAGE

Use these techniques to revise text by adding or removing characters. Ventura saves the changes you make when you save the chapter (see **Chapters**).

To edit text, you use the text cursor (or keyboard cursor), a slender vertical bar that indicates where the next keystroke will take effect. To insert the text cursor into the text on a page, you click the location you desire with the mouse. You must insert the text cursor again when you change pages or when you activate and return from another mode.

To move the text cursor from one spot to another on the page, use the keypad arrows (↑,↓,←,→). Each keystroke moves the text cursor one character; you can hold down an arrow to repeat its effect. You cannot use the arrow keys to move the text cursor from one frame to another. You must use the mouse to reinsert the text cursor in the desired frame. (The same applies to relocating with regard to Box Text.)

To insert additional text at the text cursor, simply type the text. You can also insert text from the text clipboard (see **Cut/Copy/Paste**) or from a text file directly to the location of the text cursor (see **Text/Picture Files**).

To delete the character at (that is, to the right of) the text cursor, press the Delete key. To erase the character before (that is, to the left of) the text cursor, use the Backspace key. In both cases, text that follows the text cursor (to its right) pulls to the left to fill the void. You can also delete a string of text from the page (see **Cut/Copy/Paste**).

SEE ALSO

Cut/Copy/Paste; Moving within a Document; Text/Picture Files

Selecting Text

SEQUENCE OF STEPS

Text mode
[position the mouse at one end]
[press the mouse button and hold]
[drag to the other end]
[release the mouse]

or

[position the mouse at one end]
[click the mouse button to insert the text cursor there]
[position the mouse at the other end]
[Shift-click the mouse]

USAGE

Various operations in Text mode require you to select the text that you want Ventura to operate on. See, for example, **Boldface, Cut/Copy/Paste, Fonts, Italics.**

Bring the mouse to either end of the text you want to select. You can then press and hold the mouse button, drag it to the other end of the text you desire, and release. Or you can click the mouse button to insert the text cursor at one end, then move the mouse, and hold the Shift key to click at the other end. The text darkens and you can perform the procedure you desire. If the text cursor is already positioned correctly at one end of the desired text, simply position the mouse at the other end and Shift-click to select the text in between.

Special Codes in Text

You can enter a variety of special codes into text. These codes, what they represent, and the manner in which you enter them appear in Appendix C. You can delete these special characters in the same manner that you do other characters, with the Delete key or the Backspace key. You can also make them appear and disappear with Ctrl-T, or use the Option menu and choose **Hide/Show Tabs & Returns**.

"Re-inking" the Screen

As you edit text, you may find that the text cursor erases text above or below it or that other procedures affect the screen display in unexpected ways. Often, this indicates that you need to "re-ink" the screen. Do so by pressing the Esc key.

CAP Files

When you create Frame Text, Box Text, and free-form captions for figures, Ventura creates a special file to accompany the chapter file. This file, sometimes called the *caption file*, has the same name as the chapter file, but it has the CAP extension.

You can use your word processor, in ASCII mode, to edit this file and perform other procedures, such as running a spelling check. If you do, however, be careful not to disturb the paragraph returns. Ventura uses them to determine where to place these special kinds of text.

Word Processor Text

You can use your word processor to create text for Ventura. Once you create a text file, you can load it into Ventura, adding the file's name to the Frame mode's Assignment list (see **Text/Picture Files**). You can also use preformatting to indicate which tags Ventura should assign to paragraphs (see **Tags**). In addition, when you edit the text with Ventura, Ventura saves the text in the word processor format of your choice. This means that you can use your word processor to work on the text file even after you've used Ventura on it. The Ventura document automatically reflects the changes you make with the word processor, since Ventura references the same file.

When entering text with the word processor, leave most of the formatting to Ventura. Following are some guidelines.

- Do not press the Tab key to indent the first line of your paragraphs. Let Ventura shape the paragraph by providing a first line indent when you specify that for the paragraph's tag.
- Do not take pains to create page or temporary margins. Ventura ignores the word processor's margins. Create them only as necessary for purposes of proofreading the text with draft copies from the word processor.
- Do not attempt to right-align (right-justify) or center text; the tag assignment handles these adjustments.
- Press the Spacebar only once after a period or colon. Typesetters consider two spaces after end-of-sentence punctuation excessive. If the two spaces are already inserted, use your word processor's search and replace capability to strip the extra space from the document (find two spaces, replace with one space). When Ventura loads a text file, it converts additional spaces to NoBreak Spaces, as indicated by an upward-pointing bracket ( ). Should you see these symbols following sentences, delete them.
- If you are entering tables that use tabs, do not attempt to line up the columns within the word processor. Enter one tab character between each horizontally aligned item in the table. Alternatively, place table items each in a separate paragraph, following one another, separately tagged to create items that follow left to right and then down via column tags. See **Tables** for more information on creating tables.

- Place the return that ends a paragraph right after the last period or other character in the paragraph. Do not allow an extra space before the return or Ventura may create an extra unnecessary line for text.
- Generally, press ↵ once (and only once) at the end of each paragraph, and not at the end of each line. (The exception is text in ASCII format, which utilizes a return at the end of each line and two returns between paragraphs.) Do not attempt to add additional space between some paragraphs (such as before a heading) by entering additional returns. Tags in Ventura handle the spacing between paragraphs. If there are already two returns between paragraphs, turn on Ventura's paragraph filter by entering

  @PARAFILTR ON =

  at the very beginning of the text file. This will cause Ventura to remove the additional returns when it loads the file.
- Because Ventura may remove and change material when you use a file, take care if you want to keep the file in its original condition. Make a copy of the file for Ventura to use.
- If Ventura supports a text attribute (such as underline, boldface, or italics) that your word processor creates, use that attribute only for short passages, no longer than part of a paragraph. To format an entire paragraph or more for a specific effect, especially when the effect is repeated, assign it with the paragraph tag.
- To apply a tag, enter

  @tag name =

  at the beginning of the paragraph, substituting the name of the tag you desire. No tag is necessary for Body Text. For more on preformatting, see **Tags**.
- You can enter text attributes that Ventura does not support from your word processor, as well as text inserts.

These appear in Appendix C, and the syntax is discussed under the appropriate topics throughout this book.

- To create an at (@) symbol at the beginning of a paragraph, enter two such symbols (@@). To create a Less-than (<) or Greater-than (>) symbol anywhere in the text, enter two each of these (<< and >>).
- With version 2.0, you can enter two hyphens (--) or the inch symbol (") and have Ventura automatically substitute the em dash (—, code <197>) and true quotes (“ ”, codes <169> and <170>) for these, respectively. Use Options menu/Set Preferences and set Auto-Adjustments to the " And -- setting. (You can also use Auto-Adjustments: Both, which turns on Styles as well; see **Spacing**.)
- To leave yourself reminders and comments, you can enter text that appears in the word processor but not in Ventura. This is called Hidden text. The syntax is:

  <$!*text to hide***>**

UNDO

Use your word processor's undo or delete capabilities to remove undesired material. You can also fix most effects with Ventura itself.

SEE ALSO

Tags; **Tables**; **Spacing**; also see topics for the effect you wish to create.

Text/Picture Files

You can add the contents of a text or picture file to a Ventura document and otherwise manipulate the file.

VERSION

2.0, 1.1, 1.0

Loading a Text/Picture File

SEQUENCE OF STEPS

Frame mode
[optionally, add a new frame or click an existing Empty frame]
File menu
Load Text/Picture
Type Of File: **Text** or **Line-Art** or **Image**
[specify Format, # Of Files, and (2.0 only) for text, Destination]
OK or ↵ (for the Load Text/Picture dialog box)
[use Item Selector box to select the file]
OK or ↵ (for the Item Selector box)

USAGE

Use this procedure to add a file's name to the Frame mode's Assignment list. This makes the file available for use with the chapter so you can assign it to a frame (described below).

Optionally, you can assign the file to a frame as you load it, eliminating the additional procedure. Begin by activating the Frame mode.

If you want to assign the file to a frame at the time you load it, create a new frame or click an empty frame. The word *Empty* must appear in the Current box toward the bottom of the Side-bar when the frame is selected, as indicated by black handles on the frame. (When you create a new frame, the frame is empty.) If the frame has a file assigned to it, you can empty the frame by removing the file, or you can assign the file after you load it. Both procedures are described below.

Then, use the File menu and choose **Load Text/Picture**. In the dialog box that appears, first specify the Type Of File. Use **Text** for text files, **Line-Art** or **Image** for pictures. Depending on your choice, the Format grouping will vary; use it to specify the format (generally determined by software that created the file) that the file utilizes. # Of Files is usually set for One. You can set it for Several if you want to add several files to the Assignment list; Ventura redisplays the dialog box after loading each one. (After loading the last file, click **Cancel** or press **Ctrl-X**.)

One of the choices for text format is Generated. Generated files are those that Ventura creates in the course of running the program. These files end with the GEN extension and include files created for an index and a table of contents. Version 2.0 includes the file created for printing a style sheet.

With version 2.0 only, Ventura allows you specify alternative destinations for text files. Usually the **List Of Files** button is selected, indicating that Ventura will add it to the Frame mode's Assignment list. You can also click **Text Clipboard**, and Ventura will place the text on the clipboard, from which you can paste it into a document (see **Cut/Copy/Paste**). Third, you can click **Text Cursor** and Ventura will insert the text from the file into the document, beginning at the spot where the text cursor appears.

Click **OK** or press ↵ and Ventura will display an Item Selector box (see Appendix B). Change the directory and file filter if desired and select the file you want to load. Give the OK and Ventura will load the file.

TIP

For each Format of each Type Of File, Ventura allows you to specify a directory and a file filter, which it remembers and redisplays when you load a similar file.

UNDO

To remove a file from the Frame mode's Assignment list, see "Removing a Text/Picture File," below.

SEE ALSO

Frames

Assigning a Text/Picture File to a Frame

SEQUENCE OF STEPS

Frame mode
[add a frame or click an existing frame]
Side-bar's Assignment list: *[click the file's name]*

USAGE

Use this procedure to assign a file to a frame. When you assign a text file to the underlying-page frame, Ventura generates as many pages as necessary to accommodate all the text in the file. When you assign a text file to a standard frame, Ventura displays as much of the text as the frame allows.

Activate the Frame mode. Create a new frame or click an existing frame that you want to assign the file to. If a file is already assigned to the frame, the file's name will appear in the Current box toward the bottom of the Side-bar. If the frame has no file assigned to it, the word *Empty* will appear. (New frames are empty.) Then, on the Side-bar's Assignment list, click the file's name. Ventura will display the contents of the new file in the frame, replacing any file that was assigned, and the newly assigned file's name will appear in the Current box.

TIP

If you assign text to multiple frames, the text will pick up in the new frame where it left off. Ventura will display the text in the frames in the same order as the frames are created; cut and paste a frame to change the frame order (see **Cut/Copy/Paste**). However, if you assign the same picture to multiple frames, Ventura displays the entire picture in each frame (unless otherwise restricted; see **Pictures**).

UNDO

To remove a file from a frame, see "Removing a Text/Picture File," next.

SEE ALSO

Cut/Copy/Paste; Frames; Pictures

Removing a Text/Picture File

SEQUENCE OF STEPS

Frame mode or also (2.0 only) **Graphics** mode
[optionally, click frame with the file you wish to remove]
Edit menu
Remove Text/File

File name: *[optionally, change or provide file name]*
Remove From: **List Of Files** or **Frame**
OK or ↵

USAGE

Use this procedure to remove a file from the Frame mode's Assignment list. You also use it to remove a file from a frame, leaving the frame empty. Either way, Ventura does not remove the text/picture file from the disk (but be careful with Frame Text; see "Tip" below).

Activate the Frame mode and optionally click the frame that contains the file you wish to remove. Then use the Edit menu and choose Remove Text/File. If you clicked a frame, the File Name field in the Remove File dialog box that appears will display the name of the file assigned to that frame. (With no frame selected, the field will be blank.) Edit the field if the selection is not what you intended. Use Remove From: **List Of Files** if you want to remove the file from the Assignment list. Doing so will make it unavailable for use with the chapter. Use Remove From: **Frame** if you no longer want the file assigned to the frame. (Remove From: Frame won't be available if you did not click a frame.) Click **OK** or press ↵ and the removal will take place.

TIP

You can also use this procedure to empty Frame Text from a frame; that is, to remove text entered directly into the frame, not assigned to a file. When you do, the dialog box will not appear. Instead, Ventura will ask for verification that you do indeed want to remove the text; Frame Text removed cannot be regained.

UNDO

Use the procedures above to add a removed file's name to the Frame mode's Assignment list or to reassign the file to a frame.

Renaming a Text File and Changing Text Format

SEQUENCE OF STEPS

Frame mode
[select the frame with the text file you want to change]
Edit menu
File Type/Rename
New Name: *[change name if desired]*
Text Format: *[click different button if desired]*
OK or ↵

USAGE

Use this procedure to rename a text file or to change the text format of a file. With renaming, when you save the chapter, Ventura makes a copy of the text file and saves it under the new name. You cannot use this procedure to change the name or format of a picture file.

Activate the Frame mode. Click the frame with the text file whose name or text format you want to change. Then use the Edit menu and choose File Type/Rename. In the dialog box that appears, you'll see the current name of the file in both the Old Name and New Name fields. Change the New Name field if you want to rename the file. If you want to change the text format, click one of the word processor (or other format) buttons. Click **OK** and Ventura makes the switch. The name in the Current box and on the Assignment list will change to reflect the new name, if any.

If you change the text format of a file, be sure to change the name to include the same extension as other such files. Otherwise, when loading the file, you may have difficulty finding it if the file filter is screening it out. In addition, you could confuse the format that a file is in.

UNDO

With the frame selected, use the Edit menu to choose **File Type/Rename** again. Use the same dialog box to change the file back to its original name/format. Ventura may ask for verification to overwrite the previous version.

SEE ALSO

Frames

Typography

See **Fonts; Kerning; Spacing; Widows/Orphans.**

Underline/Overscore/Strike-thru

Underline, overscore, and strike-thru are Ventura's three text lines that you control in similar ways. Ventura can underline or double underline text, overscore (place a line above) it, or strike-thru (place a line through) text.

VERSION

2.0, 1.1, 1.0 (Overscore not available in version 1.0)

Setting Text Lines with Ventura

SEQUENCE OF STEPS

To create text lines by using the Assignment list:

> **Text** mode
> *[select the text]*
> Assignment list: **Underline**, **Double Undrln**, **Strike-Thru**, or **Overscore**

(2.0 only) To create text lines by using the Set Font button:

> **Text** mode
> *[select the text]*
> Side-bar: **Set Font** button
> Overscore, Strike-Thru, Underline, or Double Underline: **On**
> **OK** or ↵

(2.0 only) To create text lines by using a paragraph tag:

Paragraph mode
[select a paragraph]
Paragraph menu
Font
Overscore, Strike-Thru, Underline, or Double Underline: **On**
OK or ↵

USAGE

These first two procedures allow you to create text lines by assigning them as a text attribute. The third method allows you to create text lines as an attribute of a tag, and so affects all paragraphs with that tag.

To use the Assignment list, activate the Text mode and select the text by dragging the mouse across it or using Shift-click (see **Text**). Then, on the Side-bar's Assignment list, click **Underline, Double Undrln, Strike-Thru**, or **Overscore**, depending on the text line you desire. Ventura will insert Attribute Setting codes at the beginning and end of the selected text that drew the type of line you've indicated.

To use the Set Font button, use Text mode to select the text. Then click the **Set Font** button. In the Set Font dialog box, change the setting for the type of line you desire to **On**. Click **OK** or press ↵.

To use a tag, activate the Paragraph mode and select a paragraph whose tag you want to use to create a text line. Then use the **Paragraph** menu and choose **Font**. In the Font dialog box, change the setting for the line you desire to **On**. Click **OK** or press ↵.

UNDO

To remove these effects, use the Side-bar's **Normal** or the **Set Font** button or delete the Attr Setting codes. See **Fonts** for more on undoing text attributes.

To remove lines created with the tag, with the paragraph selected use the Paragraph menu and display the Font dialog box. Change the appropriate line setting to **Off**.

Adjusting Line Positions

VERSION

2.0, 1.1

SEQUENCE OF STEPS

Paragraph mode
[click a paragraph]
Paragraph menu
(2.0) **Attribute Overrides** or (1.1) **Typographic Controls**
(2.0 only) Line Width: **Text Wide** or **Margin Wide**
Height and Shift fields: *[provide values]*
OK or ↵

USAGE

These settings control thickness and vertical placement of text lines that appear in paragraphs bearing the tag. They also allow you to create lines that extend from margin to margin.

In Paragraph mode, click a paragraph. Then use the Paragraph menu and choose **Attribute Overrides** (or, in 1.1, **Typographic Controls**). In the dialog box that appears, Line Width (2.0 only) is usually set Text-Wide. This means only the characters you select will receive the lines you indicate. If you use Line Width: **Margin Wide**, Ventura will extend the line(s) from left margin to right margin. This is the case even if you select only a short amount of text.

In the dialog box you'll also see fields for

Overscore Height:	Shift ↑ By:
Strike-Thru Height:	Shift ↑ By:
Underline 1 Height:	Shift ↓ By:
Underline 2 Height:	Shift ↓ By:

Provide values for the various Height fields to set the thickness of the lines. Provide values for the Shift By fields, and Ventura will use the values you indicate to shift the line up or down by that amount. Then click **OK** or press ↵.

UNDO

With the paragraph selected, use Paragraph menu/**Attribute Overrides** again. Use Line Width: **Text Wide**. Reset the original values for the Height and Shift fields. Typical values in picas and points for 12-point type are as follows: for all Height fields: 00,01; for Shift By fields, Overscore: 01,00; Strike-Thru: 00,04; Underline 1: 00,01; Underline 2: 00,02.

Setting Text Lines with Your Word Processor

SEQUENCE OF STEPS

To create a text line, as if assigned with the Assignment list:

<*code*>*[text to be lined]***<D>**

where <*code*> is as follows:

Underline:	<U>
Double Underline:	<=>
Strike-Thru:	<X>
Overscore:	<O>

USAGE

Insert these codes into word processor text to indicate text lines as if assigned with Ventura's Assignment list or the Set Font button. Alternatively, you may be able to use your word processor's procedures for creating these lines.

To indicate that Ventura should place a text line, enter a left angle-bracket (<), followed by the code listed above, and a right angle-bracket (>). Then enter the text you wish to line. To end the line, enter the <D> code. Text lines also end with a paragraph return or with another code.

If Ventura supports your word processor's ability to underline or create other text lines, you can use it instead. The effect is the same as if you use the two procedures just described. For example, with Microsoft Word, underline with Alt-U, create strike-thru with Alt-S. With WordPerfect, underline with F8, create strike-thru with Ctrl-F8, 2, 9.

UNDO

Use your word processor's delete capabilities to remove the codes from the text. You can also use Ventura's procedures, described above, to delete the text attribute codes.

EXAMPLE

To create

This is underlined.

enter

This is <U>underlined<D>.

View Changes

You can change the amount of magnification Ventura uses to display your document on the screen.

VERSION

2.0, 1.1, 1.0

SEQUENCE OF STEPS

Using the View menu:

View menu
Reduced View, **Normal View (1x)**, **Enlarged View (2x)**, or **Facing Pages View**

Using keyboard shortcuts:

[2.0 and 1.1: *optionally position mouse]*
Ctrl-R, **Ctrl-N**, or **Ctrl-E**

USAGE

Use these procedures to reduce or enlarge the display of the document. The constraints of your monitor will determine the amount of the page you can see at one time.

Using the View menu, click one of the four View settings and the view changes. On the View menu, Ventura places a check mark next to the currently showing view.

Instead of using the View menu, you can use keyboard shortcuts for all views except Facing Pages view. The shortcut code letters correspond to the first letter of the view.

Normal view most closely resembles the true size of your document, as indicated by the *1x*. Enlarged view is two times (*2x*) the actual size of the document. When you use the keyboard shortcut to enlarge (with versions 2.0 and 1.1), Ventura takes the approximate location of the mouse cursor as a cue for positioning the top-left corner of the magnified view.

In Reduced view, Ventura may *greek* some of the text—that is, substitute plain straight lines for some text—so that the program can operate more efficiently. You can set the amount of greeking Ventura performs. Use the Options menu and choose **Set Preferences**. Set Text To Greek to **None**, **All**, or one of the sizes listed (**2**, **4**, **6**, **8**, or **10**). These sizes represent the number of screen dots (pixels). Ventura will greek the size you choose and all smaller sizes.

Facing Pages view displays left- and right-hand pages simultaneously. You can use this view only with documents that have Page Layout set to Sides: **Double**. In Facing Pages View, you cannot select elements across facing pages, such as a string of text or multiple frames.

UNDO

Use the View menu or one of the keyboard shortcuts to change to a different view.

Widows/Orphans

Use Widow and Orphan settings to regulate the minimum number of isolated lines permitted.

VERSION

2.0, 1.1, 1.0

SEQUENCE OF STEPS

To set Widow/Orphan control for the chapter:

> (2.0) **Chapter** menu or (1.1 and 1.0) **Page** menu
> (2.0) **Chapter Typography** or (1.1 and 1.0) **Widows & Orphans**
> Widows or Orphans: **1**, **2**, **3**, **4**, or **5**
> **OK** or ↵

(2.0 only) To set Widow/Orphan control for a frame:

> **Frame** mode or **Graphics** mode
> *[select the frame]*
> **Frame** menu
> **Frame Typography**
> Widows or Orphans: **1**, **2**, **3**, **4**, **5**, or **Default**
> **OK** or ↵

USAGE

Use these procedures to indicate the minimum number of lines you allow Ventura to place at the top (widows) or bottom (orphans) of a page or column when the rest of the text appears on the preceding or following page (column).

To adjust the widow/orphan settings for a chapter, use the Chapter menu (or, before 2.0, the Page menu) and choose **Chapter Typography** (before 2.0, click **Widows & Orphans**). For Widows and for Orphans, you can indicate settings of 1 to 5 for the number of lines. Using 1 essentially turns the control off. Click **OK** or press ↵.

With version 2.0, you can also control widows and orphans frame by frame, overriding the setting you've provided for the chapter. Activate the Frame or Graphics mode and select the frame you want to adjust. Then use the Frame menu and choose **Frame Typography**. In the Frame Typography dialog box, you can set Widows and Orphans to values of **1** to **5** or **Default**. Set to Default, the frame uses the settings you've provided for the chapter. Set for one of the numbers, the frame uses that setting regardless of what's specified for the chapter.

UNDO

To reset widow and orphan control for the chapter, use Chapter menu/**Chapter Typography** again. 2 is a standard setting both for Widows and for Orphans. To reset widow and orphan control for a frame, select the frame and use Frame menu/**Frame Typography** to set Widows and Orphans each to Default.

Appendix A:
Installation and Reinstallation

This reference assumes that Ventura is already installed on your computer. The following is a summary of installation and reinstallation procedures. You may find reinstallation necessary if you add a piece of equipment to your system. To install new fonts, see **Fonts**.

To install and reinstall Ventura:

1. Insert disk #1 (Application Disk).
2. Enter **A:VPPREP** at the DOS prompt.
3. Follow the screen prompts.

For best performance, edit the CONFIG.SYS file as follows:

1. Using your word processor, load or create the CONFIG.SYS file on the root of the directory from which you boot the operating system (usually the C:\ directory).
2. Add or revise these commands, each on its own line ending with a ↵:

   BUFFERS=20
   FILES=20

   You can use a number greater than 20, although doing so may decrease the size of the chapters you can create.
3. Save in ASCII format.

To automatically install your bus (board, not serial) mouse each time you use Ventura:

1. Using your word processor, load or create either the AUTOEXEC.BAT file, which is run when you start the computer, or the VP.BAT file, which loads Ventura. Both are usually in the C:\ directory.

2. Add this command, on its own line ending with a return:

   C:\MOUSE\MOUSE

   Provide your actual disk drive and mouse directory if they differ.
3. Save in ASCII format.

To regain Ventura's default settings

Erase the INF files. Usually, these are in the VENTURA directory, and you can delete them by typing

DEL C:\VENTURA*.INF

To customize your VP.BAT file

1. Using your word processor, load the VP.BAT file, which loads Ventura. Normally, this file is installed in the C:\ directory.
2. Edit the DRVRMRGR line (as described below), which is a single "line," ending with a return, like so:

   DRVRMRGR VPPROF %1
   /S=SD_GENS5.VGA/M=32/X=D:/O=E:
   /I=C:\ventura\inf/A=27

   You can edit the DRVRMRGR line with the following parameters: **/S=** indicates the screen driver that VP.BAT loads, which appears in the Options menu's Set Printer Info dialog box. **/M=** indicates the port and type of mouse. The first digit is the port (0 = COM1, 1 = COM2, 2 or 3 = all others); the second digit is the type of mouse (0 = no mouse, 1 = Mouse Systems or PC Mouse, 2 = mouse using MOUSE.COM or MOUSE.SYS, 3 = Microsoft serial mouse, 4 = IBM PS/2 mouse). **/X=** indicates additional disk drives for the Item Selector boxes. **/O =** indicates the disk drive to contain overflow files. You can use this for a ram drive to expedite processing. **/I:** indicates where Ventura should store the INF files. These files store the settings in place when you quit Ventura (see **Options**). Create a BAT file for each user and you can use this parameter to store each user's settings separately. **/A=** indicates the amount of memory to be subtracted from the graphics buffer (for images) and font buffer and added to the text area for better performance. Use an integer between 1 and 32.

3. Save in ASCII format.

Appendix B: Screen Elements and Symbols

SYMBOL ON THE SCREEN	NAME IN THE CURRENT BOX	HOW CREATED
¶	Paragraph End	Return Key
↵	Line Break	Ctrl-Return
→	Horizontal Tab	Tab Key
□	End of File	(Automatically)
	NoBreak Space	Ctrl-Space
	Em Space	Ctrl-Shift-M
□	En Space	Ctrl-Shift-N
	Thin Space	Ctrl-Shift-T
	Figure Space	Ctrl-Shift-F
	Box Character (2.0 only)	Edit menu's Insert Special Item selection
	Footnote	Edit menu's Insert Special Item (2.0) or Insert footnote (1.0 and 1.1) selection
°	Index Entry	Edit menu's Insert Special Item (2.0) or Insert/Edit Index (1.0 and 1.1) selection
	Fraction (2.0 only)	Edit menu's Insert Special Item selection
	Frame Anchor	Edit Menu's Insert Special Item (2.0) or Insert/Edit Anchor (1.0 and 1.1) selection
	Reference (2.0 only)	Edit menu's Insert Special Item selection

Table B.1: Keyboard symbols

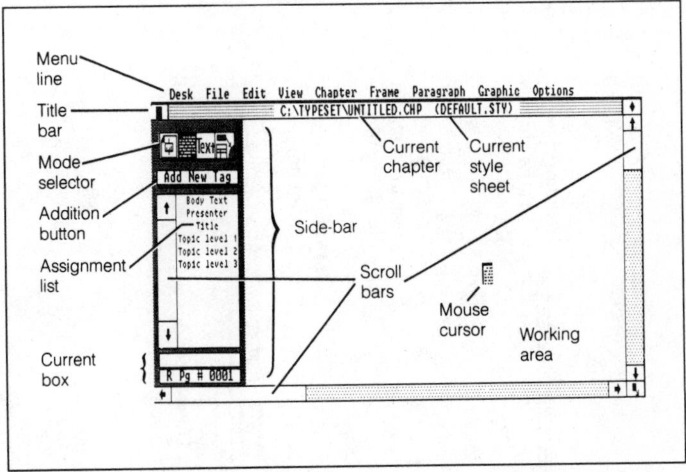

Figure B.1: The main screen

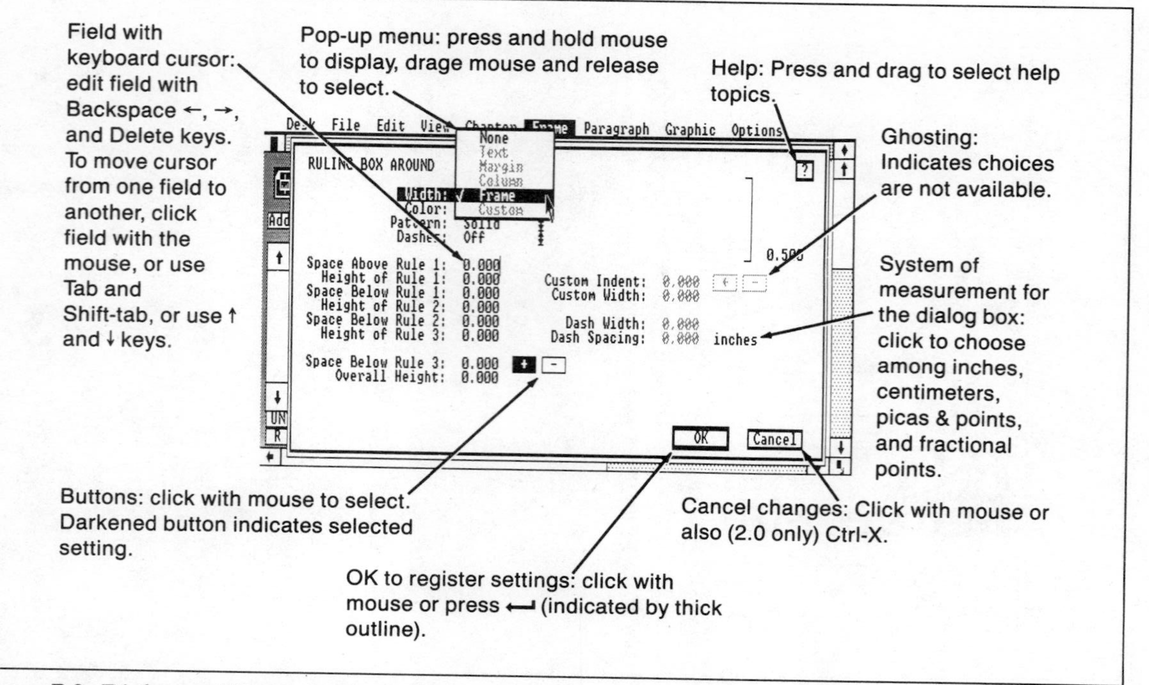

Figure B.2: Dialog and item selection boxes

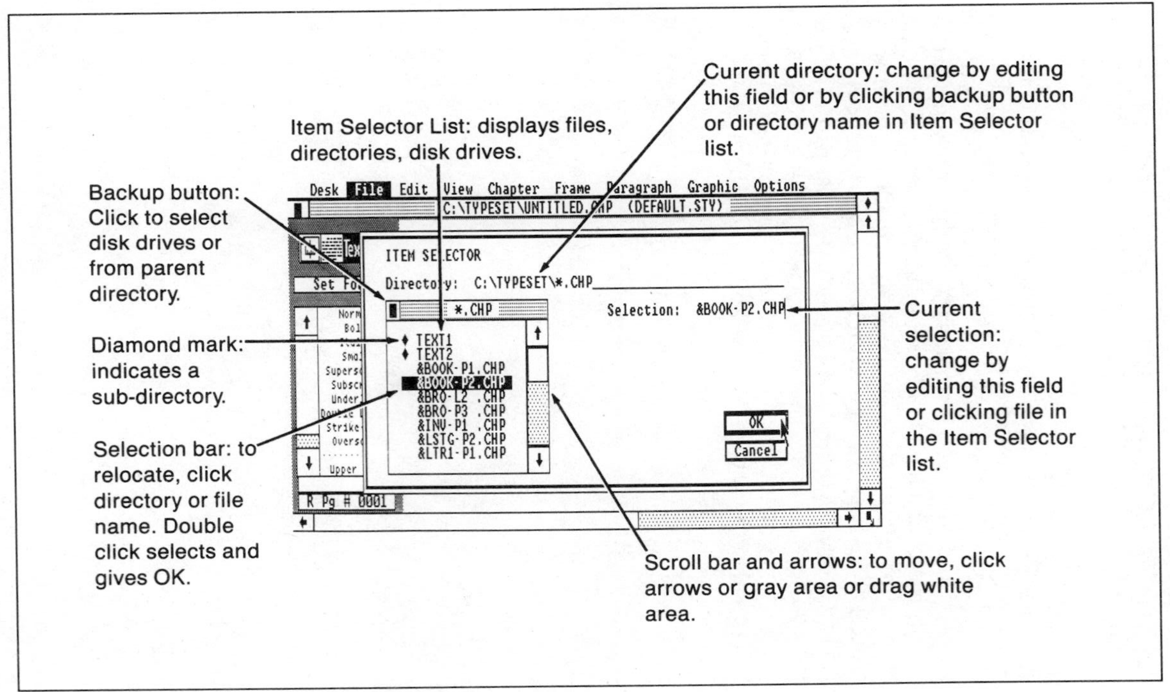

Figure B.2: Dialog and item selection boxes (continued)

Appendix C:
Special Characters and Codes

This appendix consists of two parts. The first section is a list of character sets available with Ventura. Char Set 1 is the character set that Ventura normally uses. Char Set 2 is the set that appears when you format text with the SYMBOL font. To obtain the characters, hold down the Alt key and type the two- or three-digit code on the keyboard. Or use your word processor to enter the code within angle brackets (<>).

The second section of the appendix is a listing of the text codes. These are codes that may appear in the word-processed version of your text files in order to set an effect in place. You can also insert them yourself by typing them in.

	CHAR SET 1	CHAR SET 2
1-31	not used	
32	space	space
33	!	!
34	"	∀
35	#	#
36	$	∃
37	%	%
38	&	&
39	'	∍
40	(	(
41	)	)
42	*	*
43	+	+
44	,	,
45	-	–
46	.	.
47	/	/
48	0	0
49	1	1
50	2	2
51	3	3
52	4	4
53	5	5
54	6	6
55	7	7
56	8	8
57	9	9
58	:	:
59	;	;
60	<	<
61	=	=
62	>	
63	?	?
64	@	≅
65	A	Α
66	B	Β
67	C	Χ
68	D	Δ
69	E	Ε
70	F	Φ
71	G	Γ
72	H	Η
73	I	Ι
74	J	ϑ
75	K	Κ
76	L	Λ
77	M	Μ
78	N	Ν
79	O	Ο
80	P	Π
81	Q	Θ
82	R	Ρ
83	S	Σ
84	T	Τ
85	U	Υ
86	V	ς
87	W	Ω
88	X	Ξ
89	Y	Ψ
90	Z	Ζ
91	[	[
92	\	∴
93	]	]
94	^	⊥
95	_	_

Table C.1: The Ventura character sets

	CHAR SET 1	CHAR SET 2
96	‘	‾
97	a	α
98	b	β
99	c	χ
100	d	δ
101	e	ε
102	f	ϕ
103	g	γ
104	h	η
105	i	ι
106	j	φ
107	k	κ
108	l	λ
109	m	μ
110	n	ν
111	o	ο
112	p	π
113	q	θ
114	r	ρ
115	s	σ
116	t	τ
117	u	υ
118	v	ϖ
119	w	ω
120	x	ξ
121	y	ψ
122	z	ζ
123	{	{
124	|	|
125	}	}
126	~	~
127		

	CHAR SET 1	CHAR SET 2
128	Ç	
129	ü	ϒ
130	é	′
131	â	≤
132	ä	/
133	à	∞
134	å	ƒ
135	ç	♣
136	ê	♦
137	ë	♥
138	è	♠
139	ï	↔
140	î	←
141	ì	↑
142	Ä	→
143	Å	↓
144	É	°
145	æ	±
146	Æ	″
147	ô	≥
148	ö	×
149	ò	∝
150	û	∂
151	ù	•
152	ÿ	÷
153	Ö	≠
154	Ü	≡
155	¢	≈
156	£	…
157	¥	|
158	¤	—
159	ƒ	↵

Table C.1: The Ventura character sets (continued)

	CHAR SET 1	CHAR SET 2
160	á	ℵ
161	í	ℑ
162	ó	ℜ
163	ú	℘
164	ñ	⊗
165	Ñ	⊕
166	ª	∅
167	º	∩
168	¿	∪
169	“	⊃
170	”	⊇
171	‹	⊄
172	›	⊂
173	¡	⊆
174	«	∈
175	»	∉
176	ã	∠
177	õ	∇
178	Ø	®
179	ø	©
180	œ	™
181	Œ	∏
182	À	√
183	Ã	·
184	Õ	¬
185	§	∧
186	‡	∨
187	†	⇔
188	¶	⇐
189	©	⇑
190	®	⇒
191	™	⇓
192	„	◊
193	…	〈
194	‰	®
195	•	©
196	–	™
197	—	Σ
198	°	⎛
199	Á	⎜
200	Â	⎝
201	È	⎡
202	Ê	⎢
203	Ë	⎣
204	Ì	⎧
205	Í	⎨
206	Î	⎩
207	Ï	⎪
208	Ò	
209	Ó	〉
210	Ô	∫
211	Š	⌠
212	š	⎮
213	Ù	⌡
214	Ú	⎞
215	Û	⎟
216	Ÿ	⎠
217	ß	⎤
218		
219		
220		
221		
222		
223		

Table C.1: The Ventura character sets (continued)

<table>
<tr><th>EFFECT</th><th>CODE</th></tr>
<tr><td>Color</td><td><C___></td></tr>
<tr><td>Discretionary Hyphen</td><td><-></td></tr>
<tr><td>Double underline</td><td><=></td></tr>
<tr><td>Inserted text:</td><td></td></tr>
<tr><td>Anchor</td><td><$&___></td></tr>
<tr><td>Footnote</td><td><$F___></td></tr>
<tr><td>Hidden text</td><td><$!___></td></tr>
<tr><td>Index</td><td><$I___></td></tr>
<tr><td>Italics</td><td><I></td></tr>
<tr><td>Jump of base line</td><td><J___></td></tr>
<tr><td>Kerning</td><td><K___></td></tr>
<tr><td>Line break</td><td><R></td></tr>
<tr><td>Normal</td><td><D></td></tr>
<tr><td>Overscore</td><td><O></td></tr>
<tr><td>Point size</td><td><P___></td></tr>
<tr><td>Small</td><td><S></td></tr>
<tr><td>Spaces:</td><td></td></tr>
<tr><td>Em space</td><td><_></td></tr>
<tr><td>En space</td><td><~></td></tr>
<tr><td>NoBreak Space</td><td><N></td></tr>
<tr><td>Thin space</td><td><|></td></tr>
<tr><td>Figure space</td><td><+></td></tr>
<tr><td>Strike-thru</td><td><X></td></tr>
<tr><td>Subscript</td><td><v></td></tr>
<tr><td>Superscript</td><td><^></td></tr>
<tr><td>Type weight:</td><td></td></tr>
<tr><td>Bold</td><td><B></td></tr>
<tr><td>Light</td><td><L></td></tr>
<tr><td>Medium</td><td><M></td></tr>
<tr><td>Typeface</td><td><F___></td></tr>
<tr><td>Underline</td><td><U></td></tr>
</table>

Table C.2: Codes for text effects

Selections from The SYBEX Library

DESKTOP PUBLISHING

Mastering Ventura (Second Edition)
Matthew Holtz
600pp. Ref. 581-6
A complete, step-by-step guide to IBM PC desktop publishing with Xerox Ventura Publisher. Practical examples show how to use style sheets, format pages, cut and paste, enhance layouts, import material from other programs, and more.

Mastering PageMaker on the IBM PC (Second Edition)
Antonia Stacy Jolles
400pp. Ref. 521-2
A guide to every aspect of desktop publishing with PageMaker: the vocabulary and basics of page design, layout, graphics and typography, plus instructions for creating finished typeset publications of all kinds.

Understanding PostScript Programming (Second Edition)
David A. Holzgang
472pp. Ref. 566-2
In-depth treatment of PostScript for programmers and advanced users working on custom desktop publishing tasks. Hands-on development of programs for font creation, integrating graphics, printer implementations and more.

COMPUTER-AIDED DESIGN AND DRAFTING

The ABC's of AutoCAD (Second Edition)
Alan R. Miller
375pp. Ref. 584-0
This brief but effective introduction to AutoCAD quickly gets users drafting and designing with this complex CADD package. The essential operations and capabilities of AutoCAD are neatly detailed, using a proven, step-by-step method that is tailored to the results-oriented beginner.

Mastering AutoCAD (Third Edition)
George Omura
825pp. Ref. 574-3
Now in its second edition, this tutorial guide to computer-aided design and drafting with AutoCAD is perfect for newcomers to CADD, as well as AutoCAD users seeking greater proficiency. An architectural project serves as an example throughout.

Advanced Techniques in AutoCAD (Second Edition)
Robert M. Thomas
425pp. Ref. 593-X
Develop custom applications using screen menus, command macros, and AutoLISP programming – no prior programming experience required. Topics include customizing the AutoCAD environment, advanced data extraction techniques, and much more.

WORD PROCESSING

The ABC's of WordPerfect 5

Alan R. Neibauer

283pp. Ref. 504-2

This introduction explains the basics of desktop publishing with WordPerfect 5: editing, layout, formatting, printing, sorting, merging, and more. Readers are shown how to use WordPerfect 5's new features to produce great-looking reports.

The ABC's of WordPerfect

Alan R. Neibauer

239pp. Ref. 425-9

This basic introduction to WordPefect consists of short, step-by-step lessons—for new users who want to get going fast. Topics range from simple editing and formatting, to merging, sorting, macros, and more. Includes version 4.2

Mastering WordPerfect 5

Susan Baake Kelly

709pp. Ref. 500-X

The revised and expanded version of this definitive guide is now on WordPerfect 5 and covers wordprocessing and basic desktop publishing. As more than 100,000 readers of the original edition can attest, no tutorial approaches it for clarity and depth of treatment. Sorting, line drawing, and laser printing included.

Mastering WordPerfect

Susan Baake Kelly

435pp. Ref. 332-5

Step-by-step training from startup to mastery, featuring practical uses (form letters, newsletters and more), plus advanced topics such as document security and macro creation, sorting and columnar math. Includes Version 4.2.

Advanced Techniques in WordPerfect 5

Kay Yarborough Nelson

586pp. Ref. 511-5

Now updated for Version 5, this invaluable guide to the advanced features of WordPerfect provides step-by-step instructions and practical examples covering those specialized techniques which have most perplexed users – indexing, outlining, foreign-language typing, mathematical functions, and more.

Advanced Techniques in WordPerfect

Kay Yarborough Nelson

474pp. Ref. 431-3

Exact details are presented on how to accomplish complex tasks including special sorts, layered indexing, and statistical typing. Includes details on laser printing operations.

WordPerfect Desktop Companion SYBEX Ready Reference Series

Greg Harvey/Kay Yarbourough Nelson

663pp. Ref. 507-7

This compact encyclopedia offers detailed, cross-referenced entries on every software feature, organized for fast, convenient on-the-job help. Includes self-contained enrichment material with tips, techniques and macros. Special information is included about laser printing using WordPerfect that is not available elsewhere. For Version 4.2.

WordPerfect 5 Desktop Companion SYBEX Ready Reference Series

Greg Harvey/Kay Yarborough Nelson

1000pp. Ref. 522-0

Desktop publishing features have been added to this compact encyclopedia. This title offers more detailed, cross-referenced entries on every software features including page formatting and layout, laser printing and word processing macros. New users of WordPerfect, and those new to Version 5 and desktop publishing will find this easy to use for on-the-job help. For Version 5.

WordPerfect Tips and Tricks (Third Edition)

Alan R. Neibauer

488pp. Ref. 520-4

This new edition is a real timesaver. For on-the-job guidance and creative new uses for WordPerfect, this title covers all features of Version 4.2 and 5.0 – including tables of authorities, concordance files, new print enhancements and more.

WordPerfect Instant Reference SYBEX Prompter Series

Greg Harvey/Kay Yarborough Nelson

254pp. Ref. 476-3

When you don't have time to go digging through the manuals, this fingertip guide offers clear, concise answers: command summaries, correct usage, and exact keystroke sequences for on-the-job tasks. Convenient organization reflects the structure of WordPerfect.

Mastering SAMNA

Ann McFarland Draper

503pp. Ref. 376-7

Word-processing professionals learn not just how, but also when and why to use SAMNA's many powerful features. Master the basics, gain power-user skills, return again and again for reference and expert tips.

The ABC's of MicroSoft WORD

Alan R. Neibauer

321pp. Ref. 497-6

Users who want to wordprocess straightforward documents and print elegant reports without wading through reams of documentation will find all they need to know about MicroSoft WORD in this basic guide. Simple editing, formatting, merging, sorting, macros and style sheets are detailed.

Mastering Microsoft WORD (Third Edition)

Matthew Holtz

638pp. Ref. 524-7

This comprehensive, step-by-step guide includes Version 3.1. Hands-on tutorials treat everything from word processing basics to the fundamentals of desktop publishing, stressing business applications throughout.

Advanced Techinques in Microsoft WORD

Alan R. Neibauer

537pp. Ref. 416-X

The book starts with a brief overview, but the main focus is on practical applications using advanced features. Topics include customization, forms, style sheets, columns, tables, financial documents, graphics and data management.

Mastering DisplayWrite 4

Michael E. McCarthy

447pp. Ref. 510-7

Total training, reference and support for users at all levels – in plain, non-technical language. Novices will be up and running in an hour's time; everyone will gain complete word-processing and document-management skills.

Mastering MultiMate Advantage II

Charles Ackerman

407pp. Ref. 482-8

This comprehensive tutorial covers all the capabilities of MultiMate, and highlights the differences between MultiMate Advantage II and previous versions – in pathway support, sorting, math, DOS access, using dBASE III, and more. With many practical examples, and a chapter on the On-File database.

The Complete Guide to MultiMate

Carol Holcomb Dreger

208pp. Ref. 229-9

This step-by-step tutorial is also an excellent reference guide to MultiMate features and uses. Topics include search/replace, library and merge functions, repagination, document defaults and more.

Advanced Techniques in MultiMate

Chris Gilbert

275pp. Ref. 412-7

A textbook on efficient use of MultiMate for business applications, in a series of self-contained lessons on such topics as multiple columns, high-speed merging, mailing-list printing and Key Procedures.

SYBEX Computer Books are different.

Here is why . . .

At SYBEX, each book is designed with you in mind. Every manuscript is carefully selected and supervised by our editors, who are themselves computer experts. We publish the best authors, whose technical expertise is matched by an ability to write clearly and to communicate effectively. Programs are thoroughly tested for accuracy by our technical staff. Our computerized production department goes to great lengths to make sure that each book is well-designed.

In the pursuit of timeliness, SYBEX has achieved many publishing firsts. SYBEX was among the first to integrate personal computers used by authors and staff into the publishing process. SYBEX was the first to publish books on the CP/M operating system, microprocessor interfacing techniques, word processing, and many more topics.

Expertise in computers and dedication to the highest quality product have made SYBEX a world leader in computer book publishing. Translated into fourteen languages, SYBEX books have helped millions of people around the world to get the most from their computers. We hope we have helped you, too.

For a complete catalog of our publications:

SYBEX, Inc. 2021 Challenger Drive, #100, Alameda, CA 94501
Tel: (415) 523-8233/(800) 227-2346 Telex: 336311
Fax: (415) 523-2373

MASTERING VENTURA Samples Disk

The easiest way for you to use Ventura is by applying style sheets and adapting sample documents. Now, direct from the author, you can receive a disk of professionally prepared style sheets and sample documents developed for this book's companion volume, *Mastering Ventura*.

- Samples include a resume, letter, memo, book, organizational chart, form, brochure, financial report, newsletter, table, and other formats.
- Features of the sample formats are listed and clearly discussed.
- Function keys are listed and assigned in a consistent manner, allowing you to switch style sheets easily.
- Tags are carefully organized to allow you to apply them quickly.
- Files are ready to install on your disk, together or one by one.

To order, simply fill out this coupon or send the information on a separate piece of paper. Mail to Matthew Holtz, 455 Hyde St. #93, San Francisco, CA 94109. Include a check for $20, payable to Matthew Holtz. (California residents please add appropriate sales tax.) Please allow 4-6 weeks for delivery.

Please send me __ copies of the *Mastering Ventura* samples disk.

Name

Address

City State Zip

Phone

This offer is made solely by the author, and SYBEX assumes no responsibility for any defect in the disk or program.